Whatever It Takes

The Antislavery Movement and the Tactics of Gerrit Smith

Norman K. Dann

LOG CABIN BOOKS

LOG CABIN BOOKS
Hamilton, NY 13346
www.logcabinbooks.us

First Edition: June 2011
10 9 8 7 6 5 4 3 2 1

ISBN   9780975554883

Library of Congress Control Number: 2011931231

The publisher will donate a portion
of the sale of this book to the
National Abolition Hall of Fame & Museum.

This book is dedicated to those abolitionists—
those social giants of past days—
who dedicated their resources to the abolition of slavery;
and to those who continue the fight against
contemporary interracial discrimination.

Contents

PREFACE

This book is not written for scholars of the movement for the abolition of slavery, but for the general reader who wants to understand more about one of the most exciting and consequential periods of American history: the Reform Era.

Its emphasis on the abolition of slavery allows the author to focus on one of the most significant and challenging changes of the era, and to couple the sometimes dry historical facts with the exciting and feelings-oriented arena of biography.

Gerrit Smith of Peterboro in central New York State was a powerful and perplexing player in the crusade for "freedom for all" that played out in the nineteenth century. His thoughts and actions as they related to the events of the antislavery movement can give a personal flavor to the process of reading that allows readers to feel as if they are a part of it. American history has often been presented as the glorious story of "the land of the free." Yet a major theme in the past that continues today is the arduous struggle for justice, equality, and human dignity waged by various categories of people. Smith focused on this aspect of the movement, and is seen, therefore, as a model for contemporary teaching, thought, and action.

Much research and writing has been done over the past few decades on the antislavery movement, so why another book? A new perspective on anything is always worth hearing, and as new generations of readers with widening interests arrive on the scene, a fresh look at an old issue can kindle interest in inquiry and learning. And as the spectrum of people attending college or just becoming interested in social issues widens, the relevance of historical events to current trends takes on added significance.

Years ago, an elder relative said to me, "I'm not telling you what to do. I'm just telling you what I know." Perhaps there are lessons to learn from what the Gerrit Smiths of the abolition movement knew that can help us today in dealing with the same issues of interracial discrimination that challenged the abolitionists of the nineteenth century.

~ Introduction ~

O thou chief curse, since curses here began;
First guilt, first woe, first infamy of man;
Thou spot of hell, deep smirch'd on human kind;
The uncur'd gangrene of the reasoning mind;
Alike in church, in state, and house hold all,
Supreme memorial of the world's dread fall;
O slavery! Laurel of the Infernal mind,
Proud Satan's triumph over lost mankind!
- *Timothy Dwight, Connecticut pastor and future president of Yale University (1794)*

As the leaders of the new government of the United States of America took the helm, they knew that their ship of state was not only on rough waters, but was being blown toward the rocky shoals of destruction by the winds of slavery. As an institution that contradicted the values of the Revolution and mocked the ideals of the Declaration of Independence and the United States Constitution, slavery was a cancer on the body politic.

Although many people recognized the danger in maintaining slavery, the power of the institution paralyzed most of them into a state of reluctant acceptance. A few men and women who became known as the abolitionists dared to challenge the morality of slavery and the social structure in both the North and the South that supported it, risking all their resources and their lives in the process. In 1835 antislavery journalist William Lloyd Garrison was roped and dragged through the streets of Boston as opponents threatened to lynch him. Later, he publicly burned a copy of the Constitution as a demonstration of his opposition to a government which sanctioned slavery. Two years later, journalist Elijah Lovejoy was murdered for his persistence in publishing an antislavery newspaper.[1]

In the summer of 1835 in central New York State, wealthy Peterboro landowner Gerrit Smith was trying to sort out his proper position as a player in the antislavery game when former slave owner turned abolitionist James G. Birney wrote to him to try to convince Smith to commit his resources to the antislavery crusade. Birney spoke of the political and moral contradictions:

> "The contest is becoming...one...of freedom for the <u>black</u> [and] the <u>white</u>. It has now become absolutely necessary, that slavery should cease in order that freedom may be preserved to any portion of our land. The antagonist principles of liberty and slavery have been roused into action and one or the other must be victorious. There will be no cessation of the strife until Slavery shall be exterminated or liberty destroyed."[2]

Gerrit Smith was a perplexing figure in the antislavery movement. Since his early adult years he saw America as "the home of the free, and the land of the oppressed," and was determined to use his vast financial resources to rectify injustices. But as he learned that prejudice was more difficult to abolish than was slavery, he became confused about how to proceed and changed his tactics several times over the decades. Whereas some have seen his vacillation as weakness, I see it as strength. In the face of criticism, Smith was able to see shortcomings in prevailing techniques and change his tactics. As such, he became, as one author has noted, "a good weather vane showing the direction of the ideological wind in the abolitionist movement."[3]

Smith was practical enough to try whatever it took in tactics to abolish slavery. Smith's life can be seen as reflecting the conflicted position that many abolitionists found themselves in as they fought against the vested institution of slavery. With no precedent upon which to base their actions, they stumbled over weak tactical ground in their search for a path to success.[4]

In the process of searching, Smith developed a style of thought and action that challenged traditional thought. He broke down the overbearing dualistic thinking pattern prevalent in the 1800s. Dualistic thinking separates people or issues into opposite categories such as good or evil, black or white, masculine or feminine, sacred or profane, rich or poor. Such thinking encourages dominance of one category over the other, obscuring the essential unity of both.

Because he perceived the Yin-Yang relationship between both sides of any person or issue, Smith understood the fundamental integration and interdependence of all social and physical elements into a systemic whole. This gave him a view of reality that encouraged an unquenchable optimism about and faith in each individual to opt for social justice and equality. Self-reliance on the moral being within oneself combined optimism with empathy in a formula that seemed to make revolutionary social change possible.

This vision reversed the social rule that similar people are attracted to each other, and allowed opposites like Gerrit Smith, Frederick Douglass and John Brown to work together. Because of such a vision, most of the rest of society called them "crazy" or "mad". While most people derived short-term, selfish and individual benefit from separation, the visionaries could see long-term collective benefit in recognition of the human rights of all people, and were optimistic enough to believe that others could also see it once enlightened.

As they persisted in their quest for a reformed social order, the abolitionists faced immense frustration. Whereas ideas of freedom and human rights initiated what became the United States of America, for two centuries its leaders defended a system of oppression perhaps unsurpassed in brutality by any other culture. We not only poured out indignities upon African-Americans, but also made it legal to do so. And when our own rules governing the necessity of free speech and democracy in the effort to deal with the issue of sectional differences broke down, we killed each other as a solution. Because of the prevalent dualistic thinking pattern in the 1800s, conflict was everywhere: in the home, in churches, politics, legislatures, village stores, and eventually, the battlefield. Weapons were words, ideas, whips, chains, and, in the end, bullets.

Racial separation and bias were so rigid that few people of one race identified with the other. Yet there were some—like Smith—who knew that if interracial tensions were to be overcome, a major revolution would need to occur regarding the perception of opposites in the moral conscience of whites.

Visionary leaders like William Lloyd Garrison and Gerrit Smith focused on changing the minds of those in the white community to believe that discrimination against black people was a sin, but they faced the entrenched power of religious, economic, and political institutions that reinforced white supremacy. In spite of the monumental task before them, their optimism drove them on, sparking a fire of inspiration admirable in any age, and equal to the task of persisting at all costs.

Although they eventually succeeded in forcing a change in the rules—laws—that governed interracial relationships, the social score remained the same because whites still could not identify in their hearts with blacks.

It is a tribute to Gerrit Smith that he did develop the ability to integrate all people equitably in his mind and in his community of Peterboro, New York, and it is in recognition of his ability to epitomize the goals of the antislavery movement that this book is written. Smith had a vision of what people could be, and the optimism to believe that he could, by example, foster that change toward a nation of equals.

In 1963, radical black author James Baldwin claimed that "the country is celebrating one hundred years of freedom one hundred years too soon." Perhaps as the next decades play out, we can implement the vision seen by abolitionists so long ago.[5]

~ 1 ~

The Era

When the Briton's hand was on us,
When earth trembled at his tread,
Did our fathers couch to wear the chain?
Go, ask the martyr'd dead!
The blood-stained plains of Lexington
Can tell the tale; -neath Bunker's sod
They sleep, whose war-cry once was, 'On!
For Freedom and for God!'
And has their proud blood in our veins
Grown still and cold?
Say, shall we stoop to wear the chains
They spurned of old?
—George W. Putnam, Peterboro resident

By the early 1800s the threat was clear: The entire nation would become a collection of individuals who were either free or enslaved. Surely the two conditions could not survive together.

Patrick Henry's Revolutionary War-era statement, "Give me liberty or give me death," was, in one sense, hollow. He owned slaves! This inconsistency characterized American society, and it became intolerable to those enlightened folks who saw the enslavement of the minds of non-slave owners to be as damaging to the revolutionary tradition of liberty as was the enslavement of the body.

When Thomas Jefferson wrote in the Declaration of Independence that "all men are created equal," slavery became a serious national problem. Before then it had been opposed by only a few small religious groups; now it was thrust before the public eye as a glaring hypocrisy.

The dormant forces that exploded during the American Revolution inspired egalitarianism, personal freedom, and the repudiation of absolute authority. As part of an international movement for human rights, such ideas fueled a new reform era that would be expressed through religious revivalism and political democracy.

The early 1800s opened on a new, post-Revolutionary generation of American leaders. It was an exciting and challenging time for undertaking the task of fulfilling the promises of the Revolution. These new leaders had the unique opportunity to set the shape of the American cultural future—to translate ideals into social reality. But the existing social reality they wanted to change was so deeply entrenched in racial prejudice that it made their task much more difficult than their naïve and optimistic positions led them to expect.

These optimists emerged in the early 1800s out of the Transcendentalist school of thought. Transcendentalism means simply that what is real in thought can become real in fact; in this system, the fact that a thought might contradict common experience does not mean it cannot be achieved. Such thinking characterized the abolitionists and drove their actions. They envisioned a society grounded in the empowerment of each individual.

They also believed in their ability to initiate a new social order free of oppression and based on equality and justice for all. As spokesman for the transcendentalists, Ralph Waldo Emerson saw philosophical parallels among several emerging tendencies. One was that optimism regarding possible change could drive one's ability to achieve it. Another was that faith in oneself could stimulate political democratization. There was the belief that the unification of dichotomies (rich/poor, black/white) could topple hierarchies and encourage equality. And there was the belief that the repudiation of fate could fuel individual empowerment and optimism about the future.

Finally, the transcendentalists believed that the reduction of self-centeredness would promote empathy—and the recognition that all people are interconnected.

Such thought engaged the minds of the emerging abolitionists and drove them to hard work and persistence in a cause they could not resist. Emerson admired Gerrit Smith for his lack of selfishness, his emphasis on the natural law of human rights, and his determined pursuit of equality for all. Smith admired Emerson's ability to perceive balance in nature and to transfer such thoughts into possibilities for the betterment of human society.[1]

One area of thought that paralleled the development of ideas of political equality was religion. The static, fatalistic ideas of Puritanism and Calvinism that served pioneer settlers well in enduring the worst that frontier life could offer were giving way to new ideas of individual empowerment with the advance of early industrialization and science. An evangelistic fervor called the Second Great Awakening spawned an attitude of revival across the Northeast. It was the theological equivalent of the switch from elitist, caste-based Federalist politics to popular, class-based Jacksonian democracy.[2]

Evangelist Charles Grandison Finney sparked revivals across the expanding New York and Ohio frontier. The concept of being free from the shackles of original sin fed the creative minds of young men and women to whom reform seemed inevitable.[3]

This Second Great Awakening revival spirit saw slavery as an enemy that was central to its moral fight. Slavery meant the mental debasement of a entire race due to the slave owners' refusal to educate slaves. It meant sexual exploitation and human brutality in physical punishment. It caused the breaking apart of families and discrimination based on the assumption of innate, biological inferiority.

This made a rich field of endeavor for the early abolitionists who, as 'moral suasionists', responded to slavery with moral force rather than violence. Gerrit Smith joined this early effort to change the attitudes of slave owners in the mid 1830s, believing as many did that once the moral sin of owning people as property was revealed to them, they would surely repent and emancipate their slaves.

The two major ideas that ignited this moral fight were the political idea of equality in natural law, and the evangelical idea of one's control over one's own destiny. These ideas challenged individuals to recognize the natural equality of all persons, and the political equality of all Americans. They set the stage for a social movement that would eliminate the predominance of caste over class, of ascribed status over achieved status. The obvious point was that once these principles were revealed, one person could no longer hold another person as property.[4]

The new abolitionists' unbridled optimism was well based in an innocent hope growing out of their experience with local success at changing the social circumstances of life. Westward migration to available land had provided economic benefit. Completion of the Erie Canal in 1825 had linked previously separate areas into a profitable market. Religious revivals had created new attitudes toward future empowerment and success. Political democracy was encouraging participation in decision-making processes by common people on a local level. It is no wonder that the new abolitionists believed they could translate their ideas and emotions of optimism into practical expression through the reform movement.[5]

But if the reformers were to get anywhere with their glorious and utopian ideas, the institution of slavery must first be broken.

Their optimism, however, did not serve them well; it would

take decades for them to muster the strength and to approve of the tactics for breaking down the prejudices surrounding social perceptions of black and white that justified racism.

What seemed to the moral suasionists to be a clear issue of choice was, in reality, one of a web of moral ambiguities. The Reform Era was one of experimentation with social plans and ideas. People moved back and forth across what might today seem like a boundary between idealism and real life. Utopias mixed with practicality. Dreams sweetened the recipe of reality. Thinkers became leaders as they tried to implement their visions of justice and equality.

Communes blossomed to make life perfect. Common men became uncommonly dedicated to causes to help people they would never know, and they committed their resources to programs of social change that would revolutionize life. No wonder they were seen as incompetent or fanatical! Being unsure of how to do what they were certain needed to be done, they experimented with a variety of techniques which made both their thoughts and actions look inconsistent. Dreams like the abolition of slavery, the promotion of women's rights, or temperance became not just moral slogans, but scripts for action.

Within such a setting, contradictions abounded: Antislavery people worshipped in proslavery churches; equalitarian politicians worked within discriminatory parties; traditionally second-class female citizens wore bloomers and spoke out on liberal issues in public. Millennial hopes clashed with political and economic realities. There was a newfound faith that the common man, once enlightened by reason, would do better morally. This dubious premise fueled the delusion that the popular vote could become an expression of the voice of God.

These socially vague conditions that developed as a result of the erosion of traditional institutions spawned a host of charismatic leaders whose dreams filled the void left by former certainties. Garrison, Finney, Smith, and many others with great vision attached liberal ideas to what they believed to be the universal principle of human rights. Although they lacked the institutional support for their movement that favored British reformers, they possessed enough certainty and self-confidence to persist in the face of continual criticism.

In fact, they felt secure enough to expose their feminine sides and to identify with women in a world that discriminated against them. Garrison described himself as "womanish" in his loving commitment to his family. Wendell Phillips became a permanent caregiver to his invalid wife. Smith listened carefully to the opinions of his wife, Ann. And all three men supported women's rights and fought the tide of male dominance.

This perspective showed that these men integrated abolitionist values into their personal lives. They could not help but be sympathetic to the perceptions of blacks and women, perhaps even feeling the attitudes of both groups within themselves. They merged traditional perceptions of gender and skin color in ways that threatened established hierarchies and personal desires for power, and endowed them with unending expression of hospitable emotional warmth and acceptance toward others.[6]

What they faced in their crusade was an intensity of bias that rendered the minds of those holding it inert, and mental inertia was present in both the North and the South.

In the 1820s and 30s, as human rights began to take prominence as a social issue, some northerners began to sense and voice deep-seated racial prejudices they had not previously needed to express in order to maintain white supremacy. The abolitionists' call for racial equality had awakened the dormant bigotry imprinted in the northern white mind, and in this new setting, the philanthropy of abolitionist leaders like Gerrit Smith became an important psychological and economic boost to the continuing attempts by free blacks to achieve social progress.

In the South, bias against blacks was so widespread and intense that political and economic institutions there were different from those in the North—to the extent that mutual understanding between the two cultures was nearly impossible. Southerners were caught in their own trap of a static economy and a police-state tyranny, while northerners were released to seek their full potential through their love of free labor and liberty. Even so, there was still enough prejudice in the North to retard abolitionism, and the national political power of the South allowed that region to determine much of public policy.[7]

The attempt by abolitionists to unite the North against slavery threatened urban capitalist interests that were supportive of it because of their links to cheap, slave-labor-produced, southern products. After the introduction of the cotton gin in 1793, northern financial supporters based mainly in New York City allowed slavery to grow by loaning southern planters money to plant, pick, process, and sell cotton. This left planters in debt to northern financiers; when the Civil War started, southern planters owed northern merchants over $200 million.

In 1860, sixty percent of U.S. exports came from the South, and the value of slaves was estimated at approximately two billion dollars. This figure roughly equaled the value of American manufacturing capital, so expecting southern slave owners to emancipate their slaves would be like expecting northern manufacturers to give up their machines.

The antislavery feelings of northerners were often motivated by self-interest instead of a moral rejection of racism. And the dark side of the northern commitment to liberty was that our leaders—Washington, Jefferson, Henry—were all slave owners. Still, these contradictions were unacceptable to the abolitionists, who by 1830 had begun to develop a network of people who believed that

Gerrit Smith at the age of 48 (left) in 1845, and in his 70s.

Photos from the author's collection

most other people were not honest enough with themselves to see what the abolitionists were seeing. Their world view seemed to be validated by antislavery activists like David Walker in the North and Nat Turner in the South, who were calling for violence and condemning blacks for being passive.[8]

Reactionary southerners turned their conservatism into fear and threatened the work and the lives of abolitionists, forcing them to expend their efforts on uniting the North. Abolitionists formed hundreds of antislavery organizations and supported extensive oratory campaigns in the effort to develop public support. The education of free blacks became a staple of their efforts to showcase the economic successes of blacks as a means of alleviating the fears of emancipation. Gerrit Smith supported educational institutions that accepted blacks, and he even started his own school for blacks in Peterboro in 1834.

Central New York State was an important area regarding support for interracial education through schools such as Oneida Institute near Utica and Central New York College in McGrawville. The area had become radicalized through the liberal ideas of social leaders like Smith, revivalist Finney, Oneida Institute president Beriah Green, and the migration between 1810-1840 of over six million people from the liberal think-tanks of the eastern shore states. One contemporary colleague and researcher of the abolition movement, John Stauffer, has suggested that if central New York State could have been "cut off" from the rest of the country in the 1800s, there would not have been a Civil War.

The implication is that the leaders had a high level of confidence in the possibility of sweeping change. And as their radicalism and optimism were so well connected to the rest of the North through a well-developed and networked market economy, others came to expect the immediate success of abolition by whatever means necessary—and at whatever cost.[9]

Gerrit Smith was at the center of that stage, and he contributed to the radicalization of other people and areas through his writings, his oratory, and his philanthropy. He cared so much about changing the lives of oppressed people that he spent nearly all of his adult life working for it. And it is for that reason that we should spend the next chapter examining the institution of slavery—and those who fought to abolish it.

~ 2 ~

Slavery and the Abolitionists

We may search history in vain to find a people who have
sunk themselves as low, and made themselves appear as
infamous by their treatment of their fellow men, as have
the people of the United States.... In most of the States
we are disfranchised, our children are shut out from
the public schools, and embarrassments are thrown in
the way of every attempt to elevate ourselves. And after
they have degraded us, sold us, mobbed us, and done
everything in their power to oppress us, then, if we wish
to leave the country, they refuse us passports, upon the
grounds that we are not citizens.... Their chosen motto,
that 'all men are created equal,' when compared with
their treatment of the colored people of the country,
sinks them lower and lower in the estimation of the good
and wise of all lands.
-*William Wells Brown letter to Wendell Phillips,*
Nov. 20, 1849, printed in The Liberator, *Nov. 30, 1849.*

To explain what a slave was requires a look at how he was treated
instead of what he did, because the definition is not one of occupa-
tion, but of relationship.

When labor leader George H. Evans accused Gerrit Smith of
fostering "white slavery" by holding such a huge quantity of land,
Smith called his attention to the slave/owner relationship. It was

certain, said Smith, that any person "would rather die in freedom than live in slavery—would rather starve [as] a freeman than live [as] a pampered slave." He chastised Evans, telling him that he should be "ashamed [to] have believed that the horrors + essence of slavery were to be found in any, even the most unfavorable, condition of a freeman."

As antislavery British evangelical Anglican minister James Ramsey wrote, "Had nature intended negroes for slavery... they would have been born without any sentiment for liberty."[1]

Indeed, it is the forced absence of liberty that defines the relationship between owner and slave. As Chief Justice of the United States Supreme Court Salmon P. Chase put it, "A slave is a person held, as property, by legalized forces, against natural right." The slave's life, labor, and property—if any—existed at the discretion of his owner.

The obvious contradiction between natural and man-made law prompted Reverend David Rice of the Presbyterian Church of Danville, KY to comment on the 1792 admission of Kentucky to the union as a slave state, "Either the laws of nature or the laws of man are wrong."[2]

Recognizing this contradiction in law, the Synod of Illinois proposed its own withdrawal from the General Assembly, declaring:

> Slavery is, indeed, wickedness framed by law; and as a system, is made up of such unnatural and monstrous enactments as are expressly and knowingly formed, fitted and intended to crush millions of our fellowmen down into mere chattels or property, to be bought and sold like brutes—stripping them of their rights, as rational, voluntary, accountable beings; tearing God's image out of them; sundering their most sacred obligations and relations; trampling under foot their dearest and most tender ties, and making them the doomed victims of

avarice, caprice, cruelty, lust, degradation, and moral
ruin.

This is our slavery. It is its *very nature*; its whole
tendency; its well known operation and effect and our
Assembly is fully sustained in calling it a system of
intrinsic wickedness.[3]

The obvious legal contradiction posed by the existence of
slavery led some to speak out against it. Gerrit Smith commented,
"What a wonder, what a shame, what a crime, that, in the midst of
the light and progress of the middle of the nineteenth century, such
an abomination and outrage as slavery, should be acknowledged
to be a legal institution." He saw slavery as "clearly and utterly unconstitutional," and he worked for its peaceful dissolution by legal
means. It was clear to Smith that no institution could be more out
of place, more ironic, or more anomalous to the spirit of the first
half of the nineteenth century than chattel slavery.[4]

Smith noted also that the really significant issue involved in the
slavery relationship was not economic; it was *power*. "I love slavery,"
he quipped. "It is so useful in revealing character."

William Lloyd Garrison agreed, noting that "the master passion in the bosom of the slaveholder is not the love of gain, but the
possession of absolute power, unlimited sovereignty." With racism,
as with other forms of discrimination (sexism, ageism and others), the cause is driven by the hunger for power over others. The
legalization of slavery—both by individual states and by the federal
government—rationalized that hunger.

As Smith commented, "If [slavery] can have a moral or legal
right to be anywhere, it can have a moral or legal right to be everywhere." Slavery was the statutory expression of racism.[5]

The irony involved in these early legal moves now appears clear.
The country's early leaders had established a new nation based on

freedom and liberty, and had railed and fought against those who scorned the idea. At the same time, they had built and maintained a system of oppression against those in their midst who owned darker complexions—a system that was much worse than that against which they had revolted.

Yet while they rationalized this system through their economic, biologic, and social class concerns, slavery was never completely accepted—not even in the South. Those southerners who were bothered by the moral aspects of slavery and could not rationalize its existence migrated to the North. In a Nazi-era-like exodus, the southern intelligentsia moved out. Kentucky slave owner and political activist James G. Birney; North Carolina Quaker Levi Coffin; daughters of a South Carolina slave owner, Angelina and Sarah Grimké; and hundreds of other sympathizers moved north and joined the antislavery movement.[6]

Other slave owners whose moral and economic concerns reached an impasse took the cowardly and hypocritical road and freed their slaves from their death beds (George Washington, for instance). But the hypocrisy did not stop there: the slave was robbed of dignity, knowledge, pride, aspiration, and incentive. Whites were responsible, but they blamed nature.

Frederick Douglass commented on the enormity of this hypocrisy:
> "It is only when the human mind has become familiarized with slavery, is accustomed to its injustice, and corrupted by its selfishness, that it fails to record its abhorrence of slavery...."

To Douglass, slavery was indefensible; one could not simultaneously oppose tyranny and support slavery.[7]

Yet this corrupt labor system persisted and left behind a bitter trail of evidence. Philadelphia underground railroad stationmaster William Still wrote,

"Those who come after us seeking... information in
regard to the existence, atrocity, struggles and destruction of Slavery, will have no trouble in finding this hydra-
headed monster ruling and tyrannizing over Church
and State, North and South, white and black, without...
hindrance, for at least several generations."

Still honored the abolitionist station-masters with faint praise
while saving his more fervent accolades for those who escaped:
"Such hungering and thirsting for liberty [by runaways]
made the efforts of the most ardent friends, who were in
the habit of aiding fugitives, seem feeble in the extreme."

One station-master told Still that he did not deserve special credit
for doing something that involved little sacrifice and that brought
him peace of mind. Still also noted that slaves tended to become resigned to the brutality of the system. Runaway Sheridan Ford said his
owner had treated him "rather kindly," then told of having been tied
with rope, stretched, and "whipped unmercifully."[8]

Accurate descriptions of slavery written during its reign come
only from those who could perceive its hypocrisy and brutality. Massachusetts senator and abolitionist Charles Sumner saw
"women and children on auction-block; families rudely separated;
human flesh lacerated;... labor extorted without wages; and all this
frightful, many-sided wrong is the declared foundation of a mock
commonwealth." Theodore Dwight Weld, in his study of *American
Slavery As It Is*, described the experience of the slave, noting:
"They are overworked, underfed, wretchedly clad and
lodged, and have insufficient sleep; that they are often
made to wear round their necks iron collars armed with
prongs, to drag heavy chains and weights at their feet
while working in the field, and to wear yokes, and bells,

and iron horns; that they are often kept confined in the stocks day and night for weeks together, made to wear gags in their mouths for hours or days, have some of their front teeth torn out or broken off, that they may be easily detected when they run away; that they are frequently flogged with terrible severity, have red pepper rubbed into their lacerated flesh, and hot brine, spirits of turpentine, etc., poured over the gashes to increase torture; that they are often stripped naked, their backs and limbs cut with knives, bruised and mangled by scores and hundreds of blows with the paddle, and terribly torn by the claws of cats, drawn over them by their tormentors... that their ears are often cut off, their eyes knocked out, their bones broken, their flesh branded with red hot irons; that they are maimed, mutilated and burned to death over slow fires."[9]

Iron slave collars like this one weighed heavily on slaves' necks and shoulders, causing bleeding, infection, and permanent injuries. Slave owners often herded rows of slaves—dozens in a group, or 'coffle'—for the long walk from the markets where they had bought them. They joined the collars with chains up to 100 feet long that passed through the hasp of the padlock (lower left) attached to the collar. Some slaves had to walk hundreds of miles over several weeks in such coffles.

Photograph by
Brian L. McDowell

Some did wonder how such atrocities could be defended. Massachusetts abolitionist, poet and editor James Russell Lowell pondered,

> "How could what is in its own nature the most unreasonable of institutions be reasonably defended? How could that which is founded on force and fraud be gently and honesty supported?"

Frederick Douglass wrote,

> "Slavery is a system of wrong, so blinding to all around, so hardening to the heart, so corrupting to the morals,... so sapping to all the principles of justice in its immediate vicinity, that the community surrounding it lacks the moral stamina necessary to its removal."[10]

Yet Douglass had confidence that the antislavery movement would eventually triumph as a result of a few community members who *did* see the immorality of maintaining slavery—the abolitionists. As Lowell said,

> "The efforts of the Abolitionists have drawn so much attention toward slavery, and their sentiments have found so much sympathy even in some of the Slave States themselves, that every evil, cruelty and misery belonging to the system had become painfully conspicuous."[11]

The abolitionists were not, as some of their contemporary critics believed, mad and crazy fools. They were generally well-educated, intelligent, economically secure, mentally stable men and women. They tended to live in urban areas near transportation routes like the Erie Canal that linked them with others. They involved themselves in innovative and influential occupations often related to public service, and were not opposed to adopting complex, centralized organizations as a means of pursuing long-range goals of social change. Most of them were connected with institutions of religion and exhibited a strong sense of social justice and close identification with people who were oppressed.[12]

Their piety, prosperity, and optimism combined to produce an uncommonly high level of dedication to the cause of abolition. But their goal often left them alienated and persecuted, as the general population recoiled from their efforts. Their work absorbed much of their time and resources, and they often became estranged from those satisfied with the status quo. They formed cliques that served as therapeutic units for the maintenance of their own mental health. Gerrit Smith's home in Peterboro was viewed by many abolitionists as a retreat where they could find acceptance and rejuvenation of their attitudes.

Smith defined an abolitionist as "one who is in favor of abolishing slavery, and who works for its abolition." Yet it was their work, combined with the obsession and zeal of a moral crusade, that helped to turn the general public against the few who were abolitionists. At a time when most people viewed the world from short-term local and self-centered perspectives, the abolitionists were promoting a national identity that many could not see.[13]

They were establishing new institutions such as schools, churches, political organizations, and businesses that upset old patterns. When people did business with successful abolitionist merchants like Arthur and Lewis Tappan in New York City or Gerrit Smith in Peterboro, they got a reform message as part of the deal.

These were different men, part of a new generation devoted to the public welfare through the practice of self-denial and the commitment of private resources to moral goals instead of personal enjoyment. They were men of prosperity and social position who fought for the oppressed instead of trying to use them. Men like Gerrit Smith, the Tappans, poet John G. Whittier, Theodore Weld, and William Lloyd Garrison were iconoclasts attempting to break down patterns of belief and behavior that supported slavery.

They dedicated their well-being, their fortunes, and in some cases their lives to the emancipation of people they did not even know. The fundamental difference between the Revolutionists and the abolitionists was that the Revolutionists fought for their own freedom; abolitionists fought for the liberty of others.[14]

As U.S. Sen. Charles Sumner characterized them,

> "Thus a few private citizens... undertook to grapple with a gigantic evil supported by the political, social, and business powers of the country.... They... saw the wrong clearly and they spoke very plainly."

The movement they fostered pitted passion against passion—abolitionist against slave owner—with neither listening to the other. Yet the abolitionists would not give up. Young slave girl and escapee Harriet Jacobs noted,

> "There are noble men and women who plead for us, striving to help those who cannot help themselves. God bless them! God give them strength and courage to go on!"[15]

And go on, they did—with determination. Former slave owning family member turned abolitionist Angelina Grimké wrote to William Lloyd Garrison, "It is my deep, solemn, deliberate conviction that this is a cause worth dying for...." Her passion lasted for a lifetime.

Syracuse underground railroad stationmaster Jermain Loguen commented to Frederick Douglass,

> "Had I not been wronged... I think I should have been a very still, quiet man. [But] oppression has made me mad...."[16]

Reason motivated their obsession, and they could not be silenced. Standing for the principles established in the Declaration of Independence but obscured by racial bias, they saw hypocrisy and tried to remedy it. Reason told them that natural rights came from God, and therefore were not privileges to be granted or withheld by government, not by laws issued by constituted authority or human contrivance.

As Gerrit Smith wrote, "To no human charter am I indebted for my rights." Government, he believed, should only protect and defend human rights.[17]

To the abolitionists, freedom was the strongest motivational force. In the United States, they battled a subculture that denied the rights of some through a system of bondage that reeked of bigotry, race prejudice, and inhumanity. Civil war, they claimed, had begun when slavery began, and they saw themselves as peacemakers trying to end that war. They even viewed a bloody war as preferable to a continuation of the past two hundred years of the moral and physical abuse of blacks.

It was not that all abolitionists held no prejudice themselves, but that those who did were intellectually capable of subverting prejudice in favor of notions and goals of equality. What they played out in the first half of the nineteenth century was a moral drama that dealt not with the philosophical "sin" of religious origin, but with physical and social abuse carried out with malice. Intellectual giants of all classes dedicated themselves to an ideal with a level of personal commitment that perhaps has not been seen since.

Those who fought slavery were titans whose names should glitter in gold on the walls of temples dedicated to democratic principles. But their humble lifestyles attracted little attention. Gerrit Smith—perhaps the most powerful abolitionist in the country—has been referred to as 'the most important person in American history that you have never heard of.'

Embracing "immediate abolition" as many of them did was nearly suicidal. As moral critics, they stood outside of the establishment unencumbered with concerns for their own success as politicians or businessmen, with their objective being the truth as they saw it. They were agitators exposing social corruption and inertia. In the end, their emotions and actions led to a change in the structure of society. They stirred the mire of conservatism and altered the dominant thoughts and goals of whole institutions—religion, politics, business—resulting in a giant step toward achievement of the country's stated purpose of equitable treatment of all people.

Smith once commented,

> "If this superlatively guilty nation shall be saved, the abolitionists—the men who have suffered every reproach, and every loss, and flung themselves away for the nation's sake—will be its saviors."

The techniques abolitionists employed for that 'salvation' varied widely over time. As previously mentioned, the abolitionists were conflicted over what to do in this first mass social movement in the new nation. As these young people struggled with inner conflict, each faced at some point a critical moment—a turning point—that helped to decide the issue for them. For Garrison, it was being jailed in Baltimore for having publicly condemned a slave owner. For Wendell Phillips, it was the murder of Elijah Lovejoy. For Gerrit Smith, it was the mob in Utica that prevented free speech.[18]

Following such incidents, they became more certain about what to do—and how to do it. The new challenge was in living what they believed. The job of reform started at home. For the abolitionist leaders, the true test of their commitment to the cause was not to be their posthumous judgment by historians and biographers , but the degree to which their own lives reflected the values they espoused. They tried to live out a unity between their public goals and private lives, and although their techniques for achieving this may have differed from moral suasion to politics to violence, they at least agreed in principle.[19]

As abolition scholar John Stauffer has stated well,

> "Through their example, the Smiths sought to create a diverse, utopian community whose organizing principles were love, empathy, and tolerance rather than power, patriarchy, and wealth."

The abolitionists hoped that the larger society would emulate their lifestyles. They generally wanted to create in their own communities what the communal utopians like John Humphrey Noyes tried to create by withdrawing from society. Thus the abolitionists' techniques were much more practical than they were philosophical.[20]

In the process, however, they incurred risks. At public appearances they were frequently mobbed and sometimes beaten. Their personal lives were threatened; the safety of their homes and families were threatened; their resources were always at risk. Their agitation publicized and clarified the issues in the debate over slavery, but at the cost of their personal security. Although to many opponents they seemed arrogant and belligerent, their tactics seldom went beyond civil disobedience.

In spite of the abolitionists' personal commitment to abolition, the risks incurred by their families and communities so complicated the task they faced that it is a wonder they were able to stay the course for as long as they did.

Slave Power was successfully dominating social institutions. In New York State where Gerrit Smith operated, the black population had fallen from fifteen percent in 1740 to two percent by 1850—and much of the growing white population supported slavery. This made the continuing influence of abolitionists all the more amazing—especially black abolitionists in New York such as Loguen, Douglass, Henry Highland Garnet, and Dr. James McCune Smith. What that probably indicated was the public's underlying philosophical agreement with the moral goals of abolitionists.[21]

One fascinating aspect of the abolitionist subculture that contributed to their ability to reach those goals was its in-group therapeutic value. Abolitionists had a very weak support base in the general population—even in the North. Through their frequent mutual contact, they helped one another to overcome the prejudice that had been inculcated by a racist society—a major achievement at such an early date in a society pervaded by racism.[22]

Previous to the Second Great Awakening, men often defined themselves in macho terms of patriarchy, honor, and prideful public display. The new revivalist spirit spurred some males to regard as honorable some traits that society had traditionally regarded as feminine—benevolence, empathy, and compassion. New identities were found in gentleness, self-sacrifice, intimacy, cooperation, and forgiveness. The group of abolitionists began to feel a closeness absent among most males, as the dangers they had in common brought them to fellowship.[23]

Their habit of writing to one another also sustained them in a culture of rejection. They perceived themselves as prescient leaders of a reform community that was guiding a nation toward better ways of thinking and acting. For example, many letters between Frederick Douglass and Gerrit Smith attest to their intent to provide mutual support by reinforcing a sense of optimism and purpose.[24]

Their frequent conventions and meetings were group therapy sessions that fueled their self-respect and rejuvenated their dedication to the cause. While together at conventions, they became intoxicated by mutually agreed upon probabilities of success, and once again galloped off to face the racist throngs. As one author noted,

> "These activities helped to assure members that they are part of a group with a historic mission, are not fighting alone, and have somewhere to go and others to turn to when public opprobrium weakens their dedication."[25]

Their homes—like Gerrit Smith's home in Peterboro—became havens for their gatherings; the trips they made to visit one another were more than merely planning sessions for movement activities. People attending the formative meeting of the New York State Anti-Slavery Society met on the night of October 21, 1835 at the Smith residence, having been mobbed out of Utica. Abolitionist Julia Griffiths commented,

> "I always breathe more freely in Peterboro, than elsewhere. The moral atmosphere is so clear here...."

Abolitionist political candidate James G. Birney visited the Smiths often and commented on the rejuvenating quality of their hospitality.[27]

As they supported one another, the abolitionists stood on moral principles they would not compromise—even in the face of physical and social abuse. With unwavering confidence in their rightness and a relentless faith in the power of ideas to win over the selfishness of profit, they expected to transform the established political, religious, and economic institutions of a whole society, and, in the end, succeeded in purging a social evil that contaminated the lives of every United States citizen.

In rejecting the quiet life by refusing to ignore the oppression of others, the abolitionists set the stage for the study of the meaning of skin color in American sociopolitical life. The recent expansion of research into the antislavery movement signifies the continuing relevance of the ideas of the abolitionists today. Their long-term vision of a moral society was optimistic in its empower-

The Smith mansion in Peterboro (side view) was a frequent meeting place for abolitionists, who often commented on the serenity of the grounds and of the rural community in which it stood. The mansion burned in 1936.

From the author's collection

ment of the individual. They believed it was the individual who could best contribute in meaningful ways to social change—unlike the contemporary fundamentalist pessimism that awaits the second coming of Christ as an agent of change.

It is important not to place chronological boundaries on "antislavery" activity. As a mind-set involving the opposition of all social discrimination, it transcends time and place and dwarfs the antislavery movement as but one example of a humane effort to abolish a small portion of discrimination. Even so, our study of the antislavery movement can provide valuable lessons about current interracial relationships.

~ 3 ~

Early Concerns

"We have a great work to do in our unhappy country."
- *Gerrit Smith, 1845*

There was a time in the developing colonies of the New World when slavery was considered to be a normal part of human social life. In the early 1600s when the Dutch ruled the colony of New Netherland, the Dutch West India Company imported slaves to provide labor for clearing land, building roads and structures, and fostering general economic progress.

In this seaboard colony area that later became New York City, there was little racial discrimination. Slaves were encouraged to learn skilled trades and could earn their freedom through work. With this incentive in place economic development proceeded and the colony prospered, even making profitable links to the northern frontier areas that were involved in the fur trade with Native Americans.[1]

Competition for commercial control of the New World resulted in war between the Dutch and the British in 1665-1667, and the British victory caused sweeping changes in interracial relationships. The British transformed New World slavery into a system of bondage in which slaves had no legal rights or opportunity to earn freedom, and were considered to be chattel property. The racial basis of slavery was reinforced legally as early as 1679, when British Governor Edmund Andros issued an edict that affirmed it. In 1706, the Colonial Assembly of New York made slavery hereditary by making children inherit the status of their mothers. With these changes working against incentives to improve the conditions of slaves, the economy stagnated, racial discrimination increased, and whites attempted to secure their position of supremacy by rationalizing slavery through Christianity.[2]

The result was to make slavery seem normal to white people. Slave ownership provided a lure for those who wanted to become wealthy. It offered its practitioners admiration and respectability, as well as the opportunity to become powerful and influential members of their communities.

British antislavery historian Adam Hochschild has characterized the normalcy of slavery in eighteenth century English life as akin to the normalcy of owning automobiles today: How could people possibly do without them?[3]

But slaves did not agree. There were slave rebellions in the North as early as 1638, and by the time of the first recorded slave uprising in New York State in 1712, there had been seven others in the colonies. Whites reacted to these rebellions by tightening security to maintain their supremacy. The fears that grew from slave resistance produced a police state in which whites tyrannically monitored slave behavior and passed many laws designed to maintain the inferior status of slaves. Slave revolts continued, however, with major conspiracies taking place in Haiti in 1791, and in Virginia in 1800 and 1831. Even hypocritical Thomas Jefferson—himself a slave owner—saw the danger of slavery as antithetical to democracy, as it brutalized relationships and degraded free institutions. It was a "blot," he said, on the social scene that would engender divine punishment in the form of slave rebellions.[4]

One of the first significant voices of opposition to slavery was that of the Quakers, but their concern was only lukewarm. Before

1750 they had shown little concern over slavery, probably because a high percentage of their leaders were slave owners. Early Quaker critics of slavery spoke mainly of emancipation within their own group, and they were repudiated by other Quakers for doing so. Benjamin Lay (1677-1759) and Ralph Sandiford (1693-1733) both experienced such treatment. The first Quaker group to issue a formal protest against slavery came in Germantown, PA in 1688.[5]

Two other early Quaker proponents of emancipation were Philadelphia schoolteacher Anthony Benezet and Quaker preacher John Woolman. Their emphasis around 1750 focused on abolitionism as a humanitarian reform for the whole society instead of just as a cleansing of Quaker groups. But even their efforts could not convince all Quakers of the need for abolition. In 1790 when blacks were accepted as Quakers for the first time, churches required segregated seating and set up "Negro benches" for black members.[6]

Despite the appeals by Benezet and Woolman for unity and a national focus on abolition, Quaker factions supported many different, mostly non-political and locally oriented techniques. It is impossible to generalize about Quaker abolitionist activity because there were diverse opinions in Quaker ranks. Two issues that united Quaker opinion on abolition were a general agreement on the value of the free-produce movement and on the aiding of runaway slaves. There was disagreement, however, over the support of colonization, joining antislavery organizations, and the belief that abolitionist rhetoric was counterproductive. Many Quakers feared that participation in activities related to abolition could endanger their separateness from worldly concerns and lead eventually to disunion and war.[7]

But Quakers did generally view slavery as being immoral—as stated by the 1755 Philadelphia Quaker meeting—and they at least tried to do something about it. In 1755 in Philadelphia, the Quakers made up two thirds of the membership of the newly organized

Society for the Relief of Free Negroes Unlawfully Held in Bondage, and one half of the original membership of the New York Manumission Society founded in 1784.[8]

The annual Quaker assembly in 1789 prepared an antislavery petition to the national Congress that labeled slavery as "inhuman tyranny." The Pennsylvania Abolition Society did likewise with its president, Benjamin Franklin, as signer and presenter. Both petitions were presented to Congress in February of 1790.[9]

Some Quakers did follow the lead set by the organizations. North Carolina Quaker farmer Robert Williams manumitted his slaves in the late 1700s as an example to others, and wrote the essence of the issue:

> "The Divine Law that enjoins us to do unto all men as we would they should do unto us, in its moral fitness, outweighs anything that can be advanced for keeping slaves in bondage, for while we withhold their freedom, we are in a great measure the cause, and altogether the patrons, of their ignorance, their dissolute lives and conversation."

In agreement with this theme, the 1805 annual Quaker meeting in Philadelphia petitioned Congress to prevent slavery from being extended into new territories. In 1827 Quaker leader Elias Hicks founded the Free Produce Movement to encourage the boycott of the products of slave labor.[10]

One glaring inconsistency, however, that characterized Quaker life was that because Quakers were endogamous, blacks were generally excluded from their meetings and organizations. Black abolitionist Samuel Ringgold Ward, mentored in his early life by Gerrit Smith, noted this touch of racist Quaker thought:

> "They will give us good advice, they will aid in giving partial education—but never beside their own children.

Whatever they do for us savors of pity, and it is done at arm's length."

And while visiting the United States in 1841, British abolitionist Joseph Sturge commented,

> "The Society of Friends in this country are not earnestly engaged for the total and immediate abolition of slavery.... I fear it is undeniable that... the collective influence of the Society has been thrown into the pro-slavery scale...."

Even Quaker abolitionist and underground railroad stationmaster Levi Coffin was disgusted at the lack of support for abolitionism within the Quaker religion, claiming that they had put "the weight of their influence against the few true abolitionists who advocated immediate and unconditional emancipation."[11]

Yet in spite of these early inconsistencies in support of antislavery activity, a growing number of people were becoming outraged over the abuse of someone else's rights, and were beginning to listen to "preachers" of the moral philosophy of human equality. They were challenging the norms of the 1700s when, if one dreamed of becoming wealthy, his likely role models were slave owners. Slave trading had the lure of a "gold rush."

This challenge led another British abolitionist, Thomas Clarkson, after writing a University of Cambridge prize-winning essay on human rights in 1785, to note,

> "If the contents of the Essay were true, it was time some person should see these calamities to their end."[12]

These moral revelations combined with the freedom-based, revolutionary mind-set to ignite the antislavery movement, the first stumbling manifestations of which were early laws regarding slavery.

It is important to remember that as the American Revolution for independence from Britain heated up in 1775, slavery was legal in all thirteen colonies. Realizing the incentive inherent in the notion of freedom, Governor Dunmore of Virginia offered freedom to any slave who joined the British Army to fight the American rebels. Many did so, including slaves owned by George Washington, James Madison, and Patrick Henry.[13]

The time period between the early 1770s and the early 1790s was actually one of progress toward abolition. The Continental Congress in 1775 passed an ordinance forbidding the importation of slaves. Early national leaders like Washington and Jefferson took the optimistic position that slavery would eventually expire because the system could not make a long-term profit and because it promoted moral depravity. Constitutional Convention participant and Virginia slave owner George Mason warned that "Every master of slaves is born a petty tyrant."[14]

The new United States Constitution formulated during the summer of 1787 left intentionally vague the disposition of the institution of slavery in order to ensure its ratification. But it left intact the high value placed on natural rights and the eventual achievement of social equality.

Part of the framers' problem regarding slavery was not whether it should be abolished, but whether it should even be discussed. By trying to remain neutral on the issue, they left open the question of its future development. At the same time, they laid the foundation of a power base that supported slavery through their decision to allow slave states to count each slave as three-fifths of a person. An interesting point noted many years later by Gerrit Smith was that he felt that slave states should be eager to abolish slavery in order to have their slave population counted fully (instead of only three fifths of them) for the apportionment of Congressional representatives.[15]

The optimism of this post-Revolutionary era regarding the eventual abolition of slavery was dashed by the invention of the cotton gin in 1793. The new machine increased the production rate of seed-free cotton fiber to the extent that more acreage was planted, and more slaves were needed to work the fields. The cotton gin led to the exploitation of both soil and humanity. Economic prosperity, quick fortunes, cheap cloth, greed, and avarice overrode any moral sensibility or optimism that might have encouraged earlier achievement of equal rights for blacks.[16]

Although some states did pass gradual abolition laws between 1780 and 1800, the national outlook for emancipation was bleak. The same year the cotton gin was invented, the Federal Government passed a Fugitive Slave Act allowing for the capture of runaway slaves and their return to slavery. The significance of such a move was that slavery was given Constitutional sanction.[17]

In New York state, where Gerrit Smith would be born in 1797, the prevailing attitude of the Dutch aristocracy was one of arrogance and superiority that ignored the growing support for abolition in the northeast. British author Granville Sharp noted in 1769 that slavery in New York was "notorious and scandalous not withstanding that the political controversies of the inhabitants are stuffed with theatrical bombast and ranting expressions in praise of liberty."

In 1785, Aaron Burr had introduced a bill in the state legislature for immediate emancipation that was defeated by a vote of 33 to 13; a second bill for gradual emancipation was defeated in the same year, 23 to 17. When the New York State gradual abolition law was signed by slave-owning Governor John Jay in 1799, it stipulated that slaves born after July 4, 1799 would eventually be freed—females at the age of 25, males at the age of 28. This provision allowed owners to continue to get work from their slaves until perhaps as late as July 4, 1827.[18]

While emancipation laws languished in the committees of racist legislatures in both the North and the South, it was clear that antislavery writing and organizing were gaining ground. As early as 1700, Boston Puritan and superior court judge Samuel Sewell wrote "The Selling of Joseph," an antislavery pamphlet. Quaker John Woolman wrote his antislavery concerns in 1754 in *Some Considerations on the Keeping of Negroes*, and his colleague Anthony Benezet's writings in the 1760s and 1770s were influential with British abolitionists. Rhode Island congregational minister Samuel Hopkins published in 1776 the pamphlet "A Dialogue Concerning The Slavery of Africans" that emphasized the cruelty of the slave trade, and Benezet's friend David Cooper in 1783 wrote "A Serious Address to the Rulers of America, on the Inconsistency of their Conduct Respecting Slavery." It pointed out the clash between human rights ideas and the treatment of slaves.[19]

As the nineteenth century dawned, optimism fostered an explosion of social developments that would challenge the foundations of the institution of slavery. Books and pamphlets emphasized antislavery themes, newspapers appeared by the hundreds, reform societies multiplied. At the same time, formal schooling became required in most northern states. Gerrit Smith was three years old.

Between 1816 and 1829 nine northern states established schools for young people, thereby ensuring their literacy and moral training. Reform societies sprang up to guide and advise the public on moral percepts. The Massachusetts Society for Promoting Christian Knowledge was formed in 1803, the New England Tract Society in 1814, The American Bible Society in 1816, The American Tract Society and the American Sunday School Union in 1825, the American Home Mission Society in 1826, The American Peace Society in 1828, and so forth.[20]

Other influential antislavery writing also appeared in the early 1800s. Kentucky Baptist preacher David Barrow in 1807 further popularized the natural-law thesis of equal rights in his pamphlet "Involuntary, Unmerited, Perpetual, Absolute, Hereditary Slavery Examined." In 1818 Reverend John Kenrick of Newton, Massachusetts wrote a pamphlet on "The Horror of Slavery" attracting attention to the moral issues. In 1823 New York philanthropist John Rankin's antislavery letters to his slave-owning brother were published in the Ohio newspaper The Castigator.

The first stimulation of the notion of immediate emancipation appeared in 1816, authored by Virginia Presbyterian minister George Bourne. Titled "The Book and Slavery Irreconcilable," it called slavery a form of "manstealing."

A second call for immediate emancipation titled "Immediate, Not Gradual Abolition" was authored by English abolitionist and leader in the Leicester Ladies' Anti-Slavery Association Elizabeth Heyrick in 1824. And in 1829, "David Walker's Appeal," a radical call to action against slavery, appeared in Boston.

The first book calling for antislavery action, also in Boston, was Lydia Maria Child's "Appeal for that Class of Americans called Africans" in 1833. The two most influential early antislavery newspapers were Benjamin Lundy's 1821 debut of The Genius of Universal Emancipation, in Ohio, and his protégé William Lloyd Garrison's The Liberator in Boston in 1831.[21]

As this literary activity warmed up the public's mind to the idea that some sort of action toward emancipation of slaves was needed, the first major step in that direction was the establishment of the American Colonization Society in 1817.

A closer examination of the society's mission and tactics reveals some serious moral flaws.

~ 4 ~

Colonization and Early Organizational Efforts

> As soon as I came to commune with him... to make myself a colored man—I saw how crushing and murderous to all the hopes and happiness of our colored brothers is the policy of expelling [them] from this country.
>
> - *Gerrit Smith, 1838*

In December of 1816, the Virginia State Legislature asked the governor of the state to contact the president of the United States and ask him to use his influence to obtain a place outside of the country where free black people could be sent to establish a colony. At a Washington, D.C. meeting comprising mostly southerners, the American Society for Colonizing the Free People of Color of the United States was established. Known later as the American Colonization Society (ACS), its stated purpose was "to spread the lights of civilization and Christianity among the fifty millions who inhabit those dark regions [of Africa]."[1]

The founder of the ACS, Virginia Congressman Charles Fenton Mercer, believed the society would act as "a drain for pauperism" by getting free blacks out of the United States. Even at this infant stage, the racist tones of the ACS were apparent; yet the federal government appropriated $100,000 for its use.[2]

In its early days of roughly 1817 to 1825, the ACS was attractive to those interested in the goal of the abolition of slavery. The early "abolitionists" were generally conservative, non-violent, peace-oriented persons who did not want to endanger political unity by hurting southern states or slave owners.

The society also offered a way to restore rights to Africans who had been taken from their homeland, and soothed the conscience of young liberals who felt responsible for reforming the social life of a guilty nation.[3]

The idea of colonization outside of the United States for freed slaves looked good even to leaders of the black community in the first decade of the 1800s. It was supported by such black "deans" as Paul Cuffee, a free businessman, ship captain and Quaker reformer; Richard Allen, founder of the African Methodist Episcopal Church; and James Forten, a successful Philadelphia businessman.

From his Philadelphia base, Allen had become a respected and powerful leader in the black community. He supported a scheme to send thousands of blacks to the newly established black republic in Haiti, believing it to be a Promised Land where they could assert their abilities free of racial discrimination and become politically and economically independent. When the Haitian experiment failed, many transplanted blacks returned to the United States determined to establish a viable abolition movement here. The significance of the Haitian experience was that it taught blacks that their efforts to acquire justice and equality could not be exported.

Many who joined the ACS were caught between a reluctance to upset the social structure of a budding nation and a desire to restore the 'natural rights' of slaves that they knew were being legally abused. As an apparent panacea for the young minds of future radicals like William Lloyd Garrison, Gerrit Smith, Theodore Dwight Weld, and Beriah Green, the policies of the ACS offered a temporary refuge before the storm. But by identifying with the ACS, these white men in fact revealed their own latent tendencies toward racism.[4]

It is not surprising that having been reared in a racist society, even liberal-minded people in the early 1800s harbored racist thoughts. The wonder is that they were able to subvert them to honest desires for the equal treatment of all people. But from its beginning, blacks recognized the ACS as a racist organization attempting to purge the nation of undesirable peoples in order to maintain white supremacy.

By the time the ACS was established, black leaders in Philadelphia had grown suspicious of its motives. They held a meeting in Bethel Church to protest it. Led by Richard Allen and chaired by the successful businessman James Forten, a future friend of Gerrit Smith, this anti-colonization gathering condemned the idea as a travesty as cruel as slavery itself. Colonization would remove people from their new country, split families—often for the second time, rob them of their possessions and their cultural identity, and deny them the opportunity to achieve freedom where they lived.

The meeting resulted in the publication of a protest pamphlet that condemned "the unmerited stigma... cast upon the reputation of the free people of color." Free blacks stated "that we never will separate ourselves voluntarily from the slave population in this country." This amounted to a promise by free blacks to aid the abolition movement.[5]

Even at this early stage of the antislavery movement, blacks believed that the most effective tactic for pursuing the emancipation of slaves would be to organize the masses into a popular movement that could overcome white apathy. This perception indicated their awareness of the racist intent of the ACS, and put them years ahead of the development of the mass-based antislavery social movement that would eventually succeed.[6]

As his commitment to human rights issues grew, Gerrit Smith joined the ACS in 1827, pledging $10,000 to its treasury. But even as he did so, he felt conflicted over his actions and battled with the dissonance he felt between the need for emancipation and the ACS stand that virtually ignored it. In the early 1830s, he tried to get the ACS and some newly formed antislavery organizations to work together. But he soon became disillusioned with colonization as a goal and removed his support of the ACS. This path was common to many of the budding abolitionists.[7]

Former slave owner James G. Birney chastised Smith for not putting his vast resources actively behind antislavery work, saying, "Colonization has done more to rock the conscience of the Slaveholder into slumber... than all other causes united...." Slave owners actually approved of the colonization scheme because it left slavery intact and sapped off energy that might otherwise have gone toward antislavery action.[8]

As the ACS lost favor with abolitionists, northern racism was exposed. Fearing that the emerging abolition movement might actually achieve emancipation, northerners worried about the influence of increasing numbers of uneducated blacks on their own privileged lifestyles, and they turned against abolitionists. National figures like Daniel Webster, Henry Clay, James Madison, and Andrew Jackson publicly supported slavery, thereby revealing longstanding but hidden prejudice.[9]

Some abolitionists responded by trying to prove to the mass population that blacks had the same capabilities as did whites; they had simply been squelched by oppressive institutions and prejudicial treatment. The abolitionists attempted to form schools to educate blacks: Simeon Jocelyn in 1831, Prudence Crandall in 1833, and Gerrit Smith in 1834. The Jocelyn and Crandall schools were in Connecticut and were forced to close due to local racist opposition. Smith's school in Peterboro, NY operated for only two years due to a change in his views about how best to pursue emancipation. Although important abolitionists such as William Lloyd Garrison, Arthur and Lewis Tappan, and Smith supported the schools, they did little to mitigate what had become an intense northern racial prejudice.

When Garrison returned to the North in 1830 after his jail time in Baltimore, MD, he noted regarding New Englanders that "their prejudices were invincible—stronger, if possible, than those of the slaveholders." In 1831 he said,

> "I found [northern] contempt more bitter, opposition more active, detraction more relentless, prejudice more stubborn, and apathy more frozen, than among slave-owners themselves."[10]

As Gerrit Smith searched for a new approach to abolition, he said of colonization,

> "It is... embarrassing and puzzling to those who have received the doctrine, that the descendents of Africa amongst us must be returned to the land of their ancestors."

He spoke of having "recently escaped from the Colonization delusion." He was searching—along with Garrison—for a tactic that would help Americans to recognize blacks as "brethren and countrymen." He claimed that the ACS had "ripened into the unmeasured calumniator of the abolitionist, ...the unblushing defender of the slaveholder, and the deadliest enemy of the colored race."

The Western New York Anti-Slavery Society wrote it plainly:

> "Resolved, that he cannot be opposed to slavery, who is... for colonizing any portion of the American people to a distant land because of an unwillingness to give them equal religious, political and social rights and immunities."[11]

The long-term success of colonization was minimal. By 1865, only 12,000 free blacks had been sent to Africa. As early as the

1820s the folly of colonization was apparent, and the ACS was discredited by Garrison's 1832 pamphlet, "Thoughts on African Colonization," and by the defection of major supporters like Gerrit Smith and James G. Birney. Smith commented later that "when the abolitionists fell upon the Colonization Society, it could no longer disguise itself. It stood revealed in all its grim ugliness."[12]

As the popularity of colonization decreased, appeals increased for the self-empowerment of blacks. Slaves rebelled behind Nat Turner in Virginia. Colonizationists vilified the emerging abolitionists for their desire to free black "semi-savages" and create a low class of people "maddened with the possession of the Liberty he is incapable of appreciating or comprehending." Their racism was now clearly revealed: they saw blacks, not slavery, as the problem.[13]

Another major early effort to pursue equal rights for blacks revolved around the Revolutionary period. Although their desire for political independence from Britain had driven early colonial residents to the point of war, they had not extended their passion for liberty to include black people. They were willing to die for freedom for themselves, but the intensity of racism that dominated life in the late 1700s did not allow most whites to see blacks as humans with similar needs, thoughts, and emotions.

The view held by most early Americans regarding the emancipation of slaves was that it was a private matter to be left up to each slave owner. After all, the disposition of private property was not an issue to be decided by the public. Interfering in that matter might divide people or sections of a newly developing political territory that was sorely in need of unity.[14]

Some early leaders who did have concerns about the immorality of slavery recognized the political power value of formal organizations as a technique of bringing about social change. An organization could take the fight for abolition beyond the philosophical or moral level and into the institutional level. Legislatures and courts would be more inclined to hear organizations over individuals. Organizational actions represented acceptable, peaceful attempts to pursue the emancipation of slaves in a country where slavery had long been considered normal. These organizations raised the crucial question of whether the representative government would even care about black people.[15]

The first effort in the early republic to establish such an organization occurred in Philadelphia in 1755, due to the influence of local Quakers. The Society for the Relief of Free Negroes Unlawfully Held in Bondage met in an atmosphere of conservatism, with no intent to agitate for quick social change. Known as the Pennsylvania Abolition Society (PAS), its techniques of operation gave more importance to slave owners' legal rights than to slaves' human rights.[16]

For the time period roughly defined as the Revolutionary era (1760-1830), Pennsylvania was the center of abolitionism. There was some abolition activity in nearby New York City, where the New York Manumission Society was established in 1784 with Quakers as one half of its membership. Both organizations—the PAS and the NYMS—comprised mainly conservative, elite white males interested only in gradual reform.[17]

The two organizations used similar tactics, and those tactics were generally politically oriented. They pursued legislative action, but usually with very little success because so many of the legislators were slave owners. Legal tactics were expensive and time-consuming; still, many lawyers were members of these organizations and pursued legal action—not to end slavery nationally, but to aid individual blacks in court cases. The PAS occasionally even purchased slaves in small numbers—when it would end a court battle and provide at least one person with freedom.

It is interesting to note that these 'individualistic' tactics were also attractive to Gerrit Smith. He preferred to disburse his philanthropy in ways that provided quick and tangible evidence of success. In this early stage of the abolition movement leaders seemed to respect reason over emotion, believing that human institutions could peacefully end slavery. This focus continued until about 1830, when passionate emotions over moral issues dominated for a while before institutional efforts were revived.

Another low-key technique used by the early abolition organizations was the signing of petitions. The PAS, for instance, petitioned the Constitutional Convention in Philadelphia in 1787 to ban the slave trade immediately. Its president, Benjamin Franklin, carried the petition to the convention, but when some southern states' representatives threatened to leave, Franklin did not submit it for debate.

The petition campaigns during this early period were generally ignored by representative bodies, and the response of the submitting organizations was to accept the rejection on the grounds that the country was not yet ready for the abolition of slavery. Such passive acceptance amounted to a legitimation of apathy. Petitions were treated as a nuisance and had no power.[18]

Other organizations also timidly stumbled along amid this early conservatism, actually accomplishing very little toward ending slavery. The Kentucky Anti-Slavery Association was established in 1808 and did little more than publish a monthly newspaper until its dissolution in 1822. The American Convention for Promoting the Abolition of Slavery and Improving the Condition of the African Race met annually starting in 1794, and it comprised antislavery societies from several states. Conservative tactics dominated its proceedings. In 1797 it made a lame recommendation that advocated a lifestyle for blacks that would aid them in protecting themselves from the prejudice of the white community.[19]

In summary, the philosophies and actions of early antislavery organizations were tainted by the spineless fear of upsetting social stability. The expectation was that charitable action by benevolent reformers could save the nation from the immoralities of slavery because they had the power to influence everyone. The PAS even warned abolitionists in 1789, "Be careful to join moderation to your zeal." Such warnings were sterile to the minds of black abolitionists who, by the late 1700s were making emotional appeals through narratives, pamphlets, essays, newspaper articles, and public speeches aimed at mobilizing the masses in favor of abolition.

James Forten, Russell Parrott, and David Walker wrote what Forten called "Appeals to the Heart" in their attempts to capitalize on the country's post-Revolution enthusiasm for liberty for all. Most of the appeals, however, had no impact.

It was the revolution in communications starting around 1830 that fully exposed the intensity of race prejudice among northern whites—and launched a cascade of radical action against slavery.[20]

~ 5 ~

Moral Suasion

It did not occur to us that nearly every religious sect and every political party would side with the oppressor.
- William Lloyd Garrison, 1837

When Sarah and Angelina Grimké—daughters of a slave-owner—became abolitionists, they were told by their newly adopted Quaker leaders to keep silent. They would soon renounce Quakerism and join an emerging public-speaking circuit in the mid-1830s. The conservative and emotionally sterile tactics of the Pennsylvania Abolition Society and other early organizations eventually produced dissident factions that believed quiet reform efforts were ineffective. Agitation became more important to emerging abolitionists than patience.

One issue driving this transition was whether success in ending individual cases of abuse—the old PAS tactic—should be allowed to obscure the philosophical problem of government control of human rights. In short, was helping one person more important than appealing to the moral conscience of a society that supported hypocrites committing a crime? By the late 1820s, new and young social activists like Garrison, evangelist Charles Grandison Finney, and philanthropist Gerrit Smith were searching for a way to use their resources in their pursuit of the implementation of natural

Appearing first as a seal of the Society for the Abolition of Slavery in England in 1787, this wood-cut image of a slave pleading for his freedom became famous when it was added to a printing of John Greenleaf Whittier's poem, "Our Countrymen in Chains," in 1837. It came to be known as a symbol of the abolition movement in America.

rights for all people. Although black abolitionists had been making emotional appeals for decades, they made little progress until the effort was joined by whites—a point that exposed the racist nature of American white society.

In the 1830s, the new vow was to make interracial prejudice the focus of a social war. The new tactics would include hostile attacks on slave owners, vivid accounts of brutality, and emotional mass appeals to the public conscience through newspapers and speakers.[1]

Various factors motivated people to join the new crusade, but one event that inspired emerging American abolitionists was the success of the British emancipation effort in 1833. William Lloyd Garrison and others had watched as essayist Thomas Clarkson, artist George Morland, member of Parliament William Wilberforce, potter Josiah Wedgwood and others pooled resources to mobilize the British public in their effort to abolish slavery peacefully by legal means. One of Wedgwood's craftsmen had designed a symbol for the movement (opposite page) that pictured a kneeling African in chains asking, "Am I Not a Man and a Brother?" It became an icon in the United States.

As the British antislavery movement shifted gears and speeded up in the early 1830s, abolitionist George Thompson visited the United States—including Peterboro—on a speaking tour. His appearances gave the developing American movement an aura of international legitimacy, and it gave American abolitionists considerable momentum. He noted that in America. "public opinion is... harnessing... the ignorant... oppressors of the truth in every section of this heaven-favored, but mob-cultured land." [2]

Blacks had always been motivated to agitate for freedom. They held the first National Convention of Free People of Color in Philadelphia in 1831 in response to what they perceived as rising levels of white prejudice and bigotry in the North.[3]

Whites were becoming increasingly concerned about the moral issues involved in slavery, and as they spoke out about it, they found themselves gagged by proslavery interests. The free-speech issue thus became another important motivation for joining the antislav-

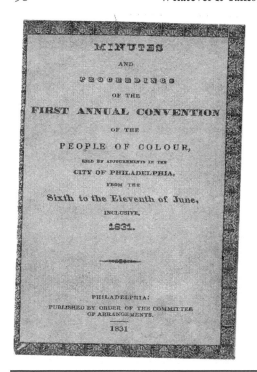

As early as 1831, free Blacks convened the first National Convention of Free People of Color in Philadelphia in an attempt to assert their rights.

- From the author's collection

ery movement. When David Walker spoke out in favor of agitation for freedom in 1829, he was found dead; journalists who wrote about black rights were threatened or killed; college students who spoke about antislavery issues or formed antislavery societies were expelled; abolitionists who spoke in public were often mobbed. Gerrit Smith's "conversion moment" occurred when a proslavery mob broke up an attempt in Utica, New York to form an antislavery society, and he delivered a stirring public address in favor of free speech on the following day.[4]

These types of issues motivated young journalist William Lloyd Garrison in 1828 to speak out about personal shame over his country's "hypocritical cant about the rights of man" while black Americans were in chains. As editor of the Bennington, VT <u>Journal of the Times</u> in November of 1828, he published a petition to abolish slavery in Washington, D.C. It declared,

"We know that the manacled slave is driven to market by the doors our Capitol, and sold like a beast in the very place where are assembled the representatives of a free and Christian people."

The House of Representatives inquired into the slave trade, and then condemned agitation to abolish slavery, claiming that slaves "would otherwise remain *comparatively* happy and contented."

Garrison called the report "The most refined cruelty, the worst apology for the most relentless tyranny." He saw prejudice against dark skin color as the supporting foundation for a slave-based society. He believed that the goal of the antislavery movement had to be the demise of interracial discrimination. Garrison imagined his wife and children in bonds and being sold and separated. This motivated him to persist as an abolitionist.[5]

William Lloyd Garrison, the founder of Immediatism, in a portrait by Joe Flores commissioned by the National Abolition Hall of Fame & Museum.

What Garrison developed was an emphasis on the need for immediate abolition. Called "Immediatism," it was a radical departure from decades of past "gradual" techniques. Garrison's logic appealed to the youthful Gerrit Smith, who also supported apolitical, non-violent action based on persuasive efforts to change the public's attitude toward slavery. Smith would eventually contribute nearly $50,000 (about $3.5 million by current standards) to the Immediatist cause.

In a culture where slavery was considered to be a normal aspect of life, this effort at change drew comments like that of New York Herald editor James Gordon Bennett that these abolitionists were "a few... crazy-headed blockheads."[6]

The fact that abolitionists tended to live sane and balanced lives in a seemingly insane society that legitimized oppression and cruelty attests to their sensitivity, personal security, and strength. They were not "crazy" or even eccentric; they were merely intense in their convictions. And they wondered why any protest could be too extreme against holding humans as property.

Garrison's choice of the phrase "immediate emancipation" may have been unfortunate because it scared many folks—both in the North and South—into worrying about their own future statuses. They were threatened by the thought of freed blacks as millions of unschooled new citizens, when existing institutions and customs were inadequate to handle them. With this threat to their own privileged positions, many whites reacted by exposing long-held biases.[7]

The Garrisonian school of abolitionists knew that full and immediate emancipation of over four million former slaves was impossible without adequate education. Still, they held to the "immediate emancipation" phrase to distinguish their goals from the older notions of gradual emancipation. Garrison called gradual emancipation "a sentiment... full of timidity, injustice and absurdity." He believed that moral pressure would change the feelings and opinion of the public to the extent that democratic leaders would eventually be forced to respond to it.[8]

The campaign for immediate emancipation was to be a secular evangelical effort—an amalgamation of the sacred and the secular. What Garrison did to make his appeal heard was to cast it in the style and language of then-popular New England revivalism. A new cultural emphasis on individual freedoms and control over one's personal achievement and destiny helped people to focus on slavery as an injustice. These new changes in public consciousness made Garrison's antislavery arguments plausible and sensible. He sought to establish opposition to slavery as the acid test of Christians' covenant with God.

Garrison's colleague, Lydia Maria Child, saw slavery as "all evil—within and without—root and branch, —bud, blossom, and fruit." She noted that the object of the immediatists' tactic of moral suasion "was to change public opinion on the subject of slavery by the persevering utterance of truth." One's acceptance of immediate emancipation as a goal was akin to a religious conversion—an ecstatic moment, a life-changing experience, a total restructuring of thought regarding human rights and equality. It represented a mega-change, and was a giant challenge to the racist attitudes of most northerners.[9]

The "truth" was based in natural law and recognized the inherent equality of all persons. "Immediate" referred to the obvious need to respond to that fact by moving immediately toward the eventual achievement of equality of opportunity for all. In that long-term process, the power of slave owners must be broken, equal protection of the law must be extended to all persons, education must be available to all, and each person must have the opportunity to be employed at fair wages. This truth was to be promulgated by persuasion—moral suasion—of pro-slavery persons to change their attitudes after they learned of the sinfulness of slavery. As John Brown biographer Louis DeCaro, Jr. put it, moral suasion

> "...was an idealistic strongly religious movement that upheld the goodness of man and the belief that selfishness, oppression, and racism could be debated, disproved, and defeated according to the sheer force of righteous words...."[10]

At this early point in his thinking, Gerrit Smith agreed with the efficacy of such an approach. He saw it as a way to achieve abolition without violence. And he realized that the need for "immediacy" was not time-based, but conceptually based as stated above. Shortly after he joined the immediate abolition movement in 1835, he wrote that although

> "we do not communicate with the slave,... if we did, we would teach him, that our hope of his liberation is grounded largely in his patience... [because] that which we seek to effect [is to be done] through the power of truth and love on the understanding and heart of his master."

Seeking a peaceful approach to immediate results, Smith sent two petitions advocating the abolition of slavery to ex-President and current Massachusetts Congressional representative John Quincy Adams in February of 1837. Adams responded that such petitions were "so unwelcome" in the largely proslavery House that its members

> "disregarded all the rules of the House relating to the reception of Petitions for the express purpose of excluding them.... I see all the individual ambition in all the free States underlined against [discussion of slavery]."[11]

While Garrison stuck to the moral suasion tactic for most of his life, Smith switched tactics as the times changed. Garrison's commitment to moral suasion as the proper technique to use in the pursuit of long-term social change was brilliant. The irony is that it could not work—not only for "immediate abolition," but for any type of abolition that would achieve equality among the races.

The brilliance of his choice lies in the fact that moral commitment to an idea underlies any person's treatment of other persons. Slavery was simply a statutory expression of racism based in white superiority, and would be maintained in some form if the *attitudes* of whites toward blacks did not change when the law did. Although all abolitionists probably understood this, Garrison and his followers insisted on sticking to moral suasion as the only effective technique of action.

Garrison's fiery commitment to abolition was ignited when he was in jail in Baltimore in 1829. He wrote,

> "Opposition, and abuse, and slander, and prejudice, and judicial tyranny are like oil to the flame of my zeal.... Am I to be frightened by dungeons and chains? Can they humble my spirit?... If need be, who would not die a martyr to such a cause?"

He appealed to conscience because he saw it as the foundation of racial discrimination and believed that it must change before racism could subside. He was right in 1829. And he is still right![12]

Garrison's colleagues in the moral suasion crusade against slavery included, in the early 1830s, almost all of the emerging abolitionists, many of whom were stable, secure, wealthy, and white. "Garrisonians," as they were called—like Wendell Phillips and Lydia Maria Child—supported him as a spiritual leader who would direct their thoughts and actions. They saw themselves as moral saints attempting to purge evil from social life, and the clique became a holy fraternity whose focus on one technique of action blinded it to the logic and practicality of other approaches to the issue.[13]

Garrison expressed this moral stand when, having received a gift of woolen cloth for a new suit, he wrote to the giver, abolitionist Thomas McClintock,

> "You have a soul capable of embracing...humanity....
> When this spirit shall universally prevail among men,
> there will be no more wars, no more slavery, no more
> injustice."

Moral urgency and purity controlled his thinking and drove him to see not only slave owners, but even those pursuing different tactics toward abolition, as wrong-headed. In an 1830 speech in Boston, he equated a "republican or Christian slaveholder" with "a religious atheist, a sober drunkard, or an honest thief."[14]

Extremist rhetoric characterized Garrison's journalism and appeared regularly in his antislavery newspaper, The Liberator. He launched The Liberator in January of 1831, and he quickly drew fire from other abolitionists who feared that his harsh style might turn away potential supporters. Such a sharp style was common with early abolitionists. Even Elizur Wright, one of the early Garrisonians, saw himself and his colleagues Theodore Weld, John Greenleaf Whittier, and Henry B. Stanton as "a pestilent, dangerous clump of fanatics... plotting freedom for slaves."[15]

At one point Samuel J. May, Garrison's abolitionist friend in Boston, warned him to "moderate your indignation, and keep more cool;... you are all on fire."

Garrison responded, "I have need to be *all on fire*, for I have mountains of ice about me to melt." He thought himself to be right in an almost absolute sense, and he refused to compromise with those who would have him tone down his rhetoric or dilute his efforts with alternative tactics. He once belittled senator Henry Clay in his efforts to negotiate compromise for "endeavoring to occupy a position half way between right and wrong."[16]

One of Garrison's major points in his argument for moral purity was that the Union would need to be dissolved before that goal could be achieved. Because he considered the United States Constitution to be a pro-slavery document, he believed it would have to be repudiated as an immoral compact before any challenges to slavery could succeed. Gerrit Smith saw a deep irony in Garrison's stand, saying in a letter to Elizabeth Cady Stanton,

> "What can they do toward overthrowing slavery, whose endeavors to that end are... neutralized by their admission that slavery can be embodied in law—real, obligatory, inviolable law [as in the Constitution]."

Garrison believed that the South was completely dependent on the North as a market for slave-produced goods. It followed that if the North withdrew from the Union and abandoned the South, slavery would dissolve. If the South depended on the North to uphold slavery, he argued, then who were the real slaveholders? His call for northern withrawal from the Union was a moral imperative designed to deliver a death-blow to slavery in a nonviolent way. Because he expected a bloody war to end slavery if disunion did not occur, he counseled,

> "...how incomparably more glorious, triumphant, and permanent is the revolution of opinion."[17]

The disunion position required that people pull away from existing institutions and build new ones based on nondiscriminatory attitudes or moral purity. Those abolitionists who disagreed with this position believed that the existing institutions could be purified by reform rather than replacement. Gerrit Smith, attracted as he was to moral suasion, was nevertheless one of those reformers who wanted to work within the existing social structure to change public opinion. Although he blamed the North for being "guiltier" than the South in maintaining slavery, he regarded Garrison's call for disunion as a rationalization of that guilt to ease northern consciences.

Differing approaches among abolitionists would eventually split the movement: the Garrisonian approach would fragment society and divide the Union, while Smith's approach would use and reform existing institutions. The former would create two separate nations, the latter a re-formed Union. For Garrison, moral purity overrode political expediency. For Smith, political expediency could hasten the arrival of moral purity. On either side, there was a misplaced optimism that any effort could alter the racial prejudice imprinted on the American mind.[18]

Such optimism was a product of the transcendental/revival era. Garrison's assumption was that if the public attitude could be brought to support abolition, Congress would respond by cleansing the nation of slavery. He even expected attitudes toward race to change quickly, and he believed—180 years prematurely—that a black president would soon represent the country. Other influential early abolitionists such as Samuel J. May and Elizur Wright supported Garrison's optimism and agreed with colleague Benjamin Roberts that "it is altogether useless to pretend to affect the welfare of the blacks in this country unless the chains of prejudice are broken."[19]

What these abolitionists envisioned was a society committed to the welfare of all. They believed this would be achieved by the sacrifice of personal or private gain by those enlightened few who could influence, by their example, the attitude of others. The error in their belief was that they underestimated the intensity of nationwide racial prejudice, and they overestimated the readiness of others to listen to their message about the immorality of slavery. Because they felt sure that they were right, they charged ahead to convince and convert others. They found that deep-seated prejudice—even in the North—prevented public approval and acceptance of them *and* their message.

An example of the intensity of this racial prejudice can be seen in the actions of the Pennsylvania Abolition Society. While it had been founded in 1775, the PAS did not have a black member until 1842, when Philadelphia Underground Railroad station master Robert Purvis joined. Following Purvis' admission to the society, local rioters threatened his home and family. His response focused not on the rioters, but on the Philadelphia community. The worst part of the experience, he wrote, was "the apathy and <u>inhumanity</u> of the *whole* community," including local white abolitionists.

The abolitionists' early naïve optimism fueled their vigor in the face of adversity. They drew huge amounts of energy from their high expectations, and this optimism shielded them from opposition. Had they understood the power of the cultural system they opposed, they might not even have tried to dislodge it. But try, they did. And in the history of their organizational activity, we can see the shifting opinions that drove their actions over the decades.

By the early 1830s it was clear to the "immediatists" that the conservative, elitist tactics of the Pennsylvania Abolition Society were not effective in changing the attitude of the general public. In 1832 Garrison, who was living in Boston, had established the racially integrated New England Anti-Slavery Society as a model for a new wave of abolition based on nonviolence and focused its attention on changing public perception. By 1833, it was evident to Garrison that it would take a national movement to do the same.[20]

In late November of that year, he traveled for six days by stagecoach and packet boat, in wintry weather, to reach Philadelphia. On December 4th a three-day meeting began to establish the American Anti-Slavery Society. The meeting took place in Adelphi

Society Hall in the black community of Philadelphia, an area that had become the focus of increasing prejudice against a rising black middle class.[21]

Of the sixty-three delegates at the meeting, one half were Quakers and a third were women. Their Declaration of Sentiments, written by Garrison, compared their quest for freedom for slaves to the Revolutionary quest of fifty-seven years earlier. But it claimed that the current grievances were more intense, because "our fathers were never slaves." Garrison pledged those in attendance to work toward abolition,

> "come what may to our persons, our interests, or our reputations—whether we live to witness the triumph of justice, liberty, and humanity, or perish ultimately as martyrs in this great, benevolent and holy cause."[22]

Some Philadelphians ridiculed the meeting as an "amalgamationist conclave," and they worried over the possibility that the new organization might actually have some influence in encouraging them to see blacks as equals. Many of the delegates reflected Garrison's radical activism and agreed with his demand for immediate emancipation. Beriah Green, newly appointed president of the racially integrated Oneida Institute at Whitesboro, NY, was elected society chairman, and he represented a new brand of activism designed to appeal to the emotions of the masses.[23]

The society printed graphic illustrations of slavery's horror against humans. It published terrifying slave narratives as serials, in public journals or as books. Society members enlisted escaped slaves to speak to public gatherings in bold, theatrical appeals for empathy and aid. This new interest in the opinion of the masses reflected a faith in democratic institutions to respond to changes in public opinion: if the old elite could not bring about change by wielding its supposedly heavy influence, perhaps the general public could cause legislatures to listen. It was, as one author has put it, "quite simply, the difference between working the courts and working the streets."

Women and blacks became more important in the decision-making process, and they were often more effective in appealing to the heart than were the old white, male elite. Mass-audience newspapers favoring immediate abolition multiplied, giving readers a sense of self-empowerment and optimism regarding the value of their own personal commitments and work. Women and blacks accounted for most of the early subscriptions to William Lloyd Garrison's The Liberator.[24]

This new wave of activity reflected a market revolution in the American public. The increasing ability to communicate among a variety of media (the newly developed telegraph and the emerging penny press) made it more likely that the greater society would share common knowledge; that made democratic participation more likely. This created an atmosphere that empowered both organizations and individuals.

Before 1830, America had been limited by cultural isolation. For two hundred years, those who had come to the new World had possessed little reading material, had seldom traveled, had benefitted from little formal schooling, and shared infrequent communication with one another. As prospects loomed for better communication and more effective social and political organizations, Garrison visited England in 1833 to investigate the British techniques that had led to the abolishment of slavery in all British colonies that same year. He found a communications network that facilitated the development of mass-based movements. Abolitionist leaders had mobilized the public; Thomas Clarkson rode the speaking circuit, William Wilberforce indoctrinated Parliament, and slave narratives appeared in newspapers.

Garrison got the message that all possible avenues of communication must be used in network fashion to muster public opinion around the rallying cry of abolition. But what he did not seem to realize was that immediate emancipation was less a threat to British people than to Americans, because British slavery was in distant colonies. Its elimination had little immediate effect on local labor relations or racist social structures. In America, the prospect of large numbers of newly freed blacks brought fears of northward migration, large-scale revolt, and a general destabilization of the status quo.[25]

Garrison returned to the United States determined to build an antislavery movement with a popular base in organizations and informational media capable of influencing democratic legislatures As of 1830, he did have a modest base of established organizations to build on, but most of them supported more gradual abolition. Most northern states and even some southern communities had organized "antislavery societies," and one national organization had been established as far back as 1794, but most of these were small and weak.[26]

Determined to build a nationwide network of strong organizations committed to immediate abolition, Garrison—through his newly established American Anti-Slavery Society—sparked an explosion of state and locally based societies. By 1835, the AASS had 225 local affiliates. By 1837 the number was over 1,000, and by 1840, more than 2,000 state and local antislavery societies existed with a collective membership of over 200,000.[27]

Much of this organizational blitz was masterminded by two AASS activists who organized an "agency system" of speakers to travel around the country to help mold public opinion in favor of immediatism. Theodore D. Weld and Henry B. Stanton had been "Lane rebels" in Cincinnati in 1834 when some students there began speaking out against Lane Seminary's proslavery position. The AASS enlisted their aid in recruiting "The Seventy"—a biblical reference to the seventy preachers appointed by Moses.

These itinerant agents became antislavery evangelicals, and as they traveled and spoke at public gatherings, they also organized people in many localities into new antislavery organizations. The AASS had made it clear that "In every village and neighborhood of our wide country, slavery and its kindred and inseparable evil, the prejudice of caste, must be discussed and dwelt on till they are thoroughly understood in all their bearings."[28]

Starting in 1836, The Seventy were selected, dispersed, and paid through AASS offices in New York City. At that time, one half of AASS income went for the support of traveling agents. Although the monetary support weakened during the Panic of 1837, some of the speakers kept at their work. The number of agents did not actually reach seventy, but was probably as high as sixty-five. Gerrit Smith was offered an agency position by Weld in July of 1836, but he declined the position. Smith did not like to travel, and often cited the "press of business" responsibilities as his reason for staying at home in Peterboro.[29]

The success of the agency system in informing and mobilizing the public throughout the North cannot be overestimated. As a component of network linkage, the 2000 or more antislavery societies that the agents helped organize popularized the abolition message and helped to create a mass attitude that favored the abolition of slavery. This developing communications network also included several other avenues for the movement of information.

Reform organizations blossomed in the 1820s during the Second Great Awakening revival. Tract societies, Bible societies, missionary societies and temperance organizations primed the public attitude for the change in morality that must precede the end of slavery. And budding intellectuals like Gerrit Smith preached that the greatest meaning in life was to be found in service to others.

This market revolution in communication also included new transportation links among formerly remote areas. The Erie Canal connected east with west through the "psychic highway" of central New York State. People and ideas began to move in influential patterns that stimulated optimism and the desire to participate in initiating a brighter future. Many lesser canals connected communities throughout the "central" states of Ohio, Pennsylvania, and New York.

By the mid-1840s, improved roads and expanding telegraph and railroad lines were moving information and people farther and faster.

New educational opportunities were creating a greater public awareness of trends, differences in people, and options for a more prosperous future. The manual labor school movement in the 1830s became a seedbed for abolitionists, as students integrated physical and mental labor with a view toward working in movements of reform for a more equitable society. In the early 1830s schools such as Oberlin College in Ohio, Knox College in Illinois, Oneida Institute in Central New York, and even Gerrit Smith's small school in Peterboro offered instruction in techniques for moral change to classes that were usually racially integrated.

The Lyceum movement in the 1820s and 1830s also contributed to the education and general stimulation of the public mind. Information-hungry people in thousands of local communities welcomed traveling lecturers to enlighten them on many subjects, including antislavery ideas.

One important aspect of the Lyceum movement was its tendency to attract and educate women, who were more likely than men to transfer to an entire family what they had learned. To educate a man was to educate a worker; to educate a woman was to educate a family. And if abolition was the message—as it often was—then women often took that message far beyond the lecture hall.

The messengers themselves could be role models for emerging activists. Black speakers such as Martin Delany, James McCune

Smith, Henry Highland Garnet, and Frederick Douglass undoubt-
edly motivated many others. Their message was not utopian; they
advocated battling against discrimination, oppression, and exploitation.[30]

Adding to the intellectual fodder for hungry minds was the
growing contribution of the print media. Book publishing became
an important source of information. One of the most significant
early publications was Theodore Weld's "American Slavery As It Is"
in 1839. He presented the brutal horror of slavery with such clarity
that there was no effective counteracting response to it.

The emergence of the cylinder press in the early 1840s made
newspapers available and affordable in unprecedented numbers to
the general public in a movement that came to be known as the
'penny press'. The new mass-production technique had a similar
effect on book printing: more than 20,000 impressions could be
produced per hour at a relatively low price, thereby making books
more readily available to the masses. When Harriet Beecher Stowe
published "Uncle Tom's Cabin" in 1852, so many people read it
that it was an effective recruiting tool for the antislavery movement.
Stowe used factual examples from Weld's book and from personal
accounts of underground railroad stationmasters—one of whom
was Gerrit Smith—to write a fictional account of slavery.

Over four million copies of her book were eventually sold to a
nationwide readership of approximately fifteen million people. The
irony was that the truth about slavery, told in slave narratives or related by hundreds of traveling speakers and in dozens of antislavery
newspapers, could not convince northerners to embrace abolition.
A fictional story did just that.[31]

Antislavery newspapers became a major source of information, propaganda, and communication linkage between 1830 and
1860. William Lloyd Garrison inaugurated The Liberator in 1831
after having worked in 1828 as editor of Journal of the Times in

Bennington, Vermont, and working as apprentice in 1829 to the Genius of Universal Emancipation editor Benjamin Lundy. Garrison started his own paper in part because Lundy was not radical enough to suit him. Even though Garrison's invective rhetoric often worried other antislavery activists, he pressed on, becoming a major force in shaping early antislavery tactics.

Most of the early subscribers to The Liberator were black, and they clearly understood that only a radical stand could change the moral orientation of white slave owners. To black abolitionist leader James McCune Smith, it appeared that Garrison was patronizing blacks in his effort to get them to join the AASS and subscribe to The Liberator. But in truth, blacks were probably just more sensitive to Garrison's radical approach. By the end of the decade there were over seventy antislavery newspapers in the free states.[32]

When Frederick Douglass moved from Massachusetts to Rochester, NY in 1847, it was in part to escape the influence of Garrison and his moral suasion approach to abolition. With financial help from Gerrit Smith, Douglass established his own newspaper, The North Star. It merged with the Liberty Party Paper in 1851 to become Frederick Douglass' Paper, and he continued to publish it into the 1860s with growing emphasis on political activity. Smith continued his financial support throughout Douglass' journalistic efforts, but Douglass avoided any public recognition of Smith's support due to his fear of offending potential subscribers.[33]

The invention of the steam-powered printing press in the mid-1830s had allowed a huge increase in the previous volume of printed items available. The AASS issued over a million printed items—books, pamphlets, tracts, circulars, newspapers—between May 1835 and May 1836. Many of these printed pieces were mailed all over the country in a "postal campaign" to support the antislavery movement. In the two years of 1835-1837, over one million pieces of antislavery literature went out.[34]

What all these communication links produced was a networked cadre of highly diverse workers that included social leaders, government officials, businessmen, newspaper publishers and editors, Quakers, philosophers, Free-Church people, blacks, women—in other words, a cross-section of a democratic population that could act as a fairly stable foundation for a social movement.

It even united seemingly opposed causes in support of abolition: religion and politics in the Free Church; politics and economics in the boycott of slave labor products; class distinction and community commitment in the underground railroad. Certainly one of the most important accomplishments of this new network was the involvement of women in antislavery work.

The Reform Era represented a new age in which the power to bring about social change was spreading to all people. As individual self-empowerment became possible, women began to escape from their male-woven cocoons and develop wings of independence. As one woman queried in The Liberator:

"Wake up, wake up, and be alive,
Let the subject of the day revive!
How can you sleep, how can you be at rest,
And never pity the oppressed[?]"

Women were indeed oppressed by the male-dominated culture of the nineteenth century. They could not vote and had few of the legal rights except as they were appended to men. It is no wonder that not many women got involved in social issues. Their courage was lacking, and their enthusiasm was squelched by prevailing norms. Even Lydia Maria Child, a well-known and well-read author and editor in the antislavery movement, thought of herself as a sideline figure:

"Oh, if I was a man, how I *would* lecture! But I am a woman, and so I sit in the corner and knit socks."

Yet it was the antislavery movement that gave women the opportunity to emerge as important sociopolitical figures. Child was not pleased with the segregation of women in the movement:
> "I have never very earnestly entered into the plan of female conventions and societies. They always seemed to me like half a pair of scissors...."

When she did join the Boston Female Anti-Slavery Society in 1834, she was ridiculed by the local press as a "petticoat politician."[35]

The women's rights movement should not be seen as just a peripheral offshoot of the antislavery movement. Although many male abolitionists treated women as inferior and expected them to request permission to participate, some male leaders of the antislavery movement recognized the participation of women as an important element in its success. Gerrit Smith argued that women should have equal power with men in discussions and decision-making during antislavery meetings.

Garrison noted that "the Anti-Slavery cause... [is indebted to] the efforts and sacrifices of the women who helped it...."

Frederick Douglass said that women provided the "deep moral convictions" that helped keep the movement going in difficult times.[36]

Statements about the moral concerns of women being higher than those of men in mid-nineteenth century America may just reflect the limited issues that women were allowed by men to deal with. Because women were discouraged from political and economic activity, they took up the temperance cause and participated in revivals of religion. Those men who could consider and master traditionally feminine roles, and were personally stable enough to handle the public rebuke, were also committed to temperance. Gerrit Smith, for instance, championed temperance throughout his life.

Women's involvement in the temperance movement did not challenge the boundaries of what society dictated they should be concerned about, but abolition did; after 1840, the techniques of pursuing it had become very political. In the same way that racism prevented blacks from participating in society, gender bias by white males prevented most women from joining the fight for the abolition of slavery. White males were known to attack politically active women by mobbing their antislavery meetings.

One of the stronger incentives for a woman to become recognized as an abolitionist was the opportunity to develop an identity other than that of a domestic servant to a male. Rather than being seen as one who sewed, cooked, knitted and otherwise kept silent, a woman could join the political world, speak in public, develop collective strength in organizations, have influence on contemporary issues, and feel a sense of self-empowerment and distinction. As "sisters" in bonds, some women developed a sense of shared moral duty to help others who were also oppressed.[37]

When Angelina Grimké—daughter of a southern slave owner—moved to Philadelphia and became an outspoken abolitionist in 1837, she threatened the male power structure of the abolition movement by highlighting the discriminatory behavior of males that oppressed women. Threatened by the revelation of their own hypocrisy, some men tried to silence her, but they could not. Angelina pointed out to women that they as well as blacks had been "accused of mental inferiority, and denied the privileges of a liberal education."[38]

Elizabeth Chandler, a white woman from Delaware, advocated abolitionist leadership by women in the early 1830s. Maria W. Stewart, a black woman from Boston, in 1833 publicly emphasized the need for black women to become involved in the fight for equal rights.[39]

Elizabeth Cady, Gerrit Smith's first cousin, attributed her early interest in human rights issues to visits with the Smith family home in Peterboro during the 1830s. Her biographer notes,

> "At Peterboro, [she] met Oneida Indians.... Her visits made her receptive to the reform spirit. She was challenged to think about issues... And... thrived on the... exchange of ideas."[40]

The Oneida Indians were an early connection in Gerrit Smith's life, and they probably modeled for him some important lessons regarding the distribution of social power in human life. Gerrit's father, Peter, had close contact with the Oneidas during his early business dealings with them in the fur trade, and they were often visitors to his Peterboro home when Gerrit was a young boy.

The Oneida social structure was gynocratic—a form which recognizes the natural power of women and accepts the differences among people that produce social balance and stability. Smith's contact early in life with this gender-power reversal of traditional European male dominance models may have conditioned his sensitivity to human rights issues. As a young adult, he identified closely with his mother, but not with his father.[41]

Gynocracy characterized about seventy percent of native North American tribes, in which women wielded economic and decision-making power. They acquired this power naturally through their biological ability to reproduce and thereby perpetuate the human family. Without this function life would cease, so women were seen as the 'life givers' to both individuals and society. Within a gynocracy it was an honor to be able to successfully mimic a woman, so male cross-dressers were idolized, but did not thereby acquire power. Pseudo-power accrued to men who became chiefs, but it was limited to legitimizing decisions made by women.[42]

The gynocratic model for a balanced, just, and equitable society has been ignored by the writers of history, who usually were of European, Middle-Eastern, or Latin decent and had no cultural background for understanding the significance of feminine power. They tended to see cultures like the Oneidas as ignorant or backwards. Those women who did challenge the legitimacy of this stereotype were seen as deviants; in order to be accepted, they had to somehow be masculinized. An example was John Brown's labeling of Harriet Tubman as "General Tubman."[43]

When male arrogance opposed political activity by women, they responded by establishing female anti-slavery societies. The first was organized in 1832 by black women in Salem, Massachusetts; over the next decade, hundreds more were established at state and local levels. The new female political culture was also nurtured through annual antislavery conventions of women during the late 1830s. Held in nationally prominent cities like New York and Philadelphia, the conventions provided visibility and legitimacy to the women's effort. Even so, those who participated in political activity faced the ire of the male-dominated society in the form of reproach, ridicule, rudeness, persecution, and violence.[44]

Elizabeth Cady had been primed for the fight in part by her cousin, Gerrit Smith. She was ready by 1840 when she married Henry B. Stanton to do her part in bringing about a 'quasi-gynocracy' that did not imply domination by men or women, but rather an equalization of power that would encourage the eventual achievement of equal rights for both women and blacks.

Women who became involved in human rights reforms had to become well-informed and effective agents of action in order to enter the developing political and economic marketplace. They ignored warnings from men to be silent. Abolitionist Abby Kelley at the Lynn, Massachusetts Female Anti-Slavery Society meeting in 1837 offered a resolution encouraging members to be active in "coming forward and communicating our thoughts unreservedly."[45]

In January of 1832, William Lloyd Garrison added a "Ladies Department" to The Liberator that printed articles designed to teach women how to participate effectively in the antislavery movement. They were encouraged to learn how to speak and debate in public, challenge class and gender limitations, be confrontational to authority, and alter their self-perceptions. Most of their work, however, seemed menial compared to that of men who were traveling lecturers or national political figures. And Garrison did not seem to understand that relegating women's concerns to a separate section of his paper was, itself, discriminatory.

Much of the women's work included fund-raising through antislavery fairs, sponsoring and organizing lectures and educational events, and writing letters and diaries. Between 1836 and 1852, the Philadelphia Female Anti-Slavery Society donated $13,845 to male-dominated antislavery organizations. The December 1854 Anti-Slavery Fair in Philadelphia raised $2,192.38—the equivalent of more than $164,000 in today's terms. In some years, women accounted for as much as 45 percent of all donations. But because they could not vote, their only means of breaking into the political arena was through petitions.[46]

It must be noted that women performed antislavery in addition to their normally expected duties as housewives and mothers. Circulating antislavery petitions was generally viewed as a time-consuming, frustrating, and disagreeable task, but women persisted at it. At the second Anti-Slavery Convention of American Women in 1838, Angelina Grimké warned,

> "It is only though our petitions that you can reach the Legislature. It is, therefore, peculiarly your duty to petition."

It is estimated that by 1840, 415,000 petitions had been submitted to members of Congress.[47]

At that point, two problems arose. First, the glut of petitions clogged the legislative operations of the House of Representatives. More importantly, southern Congressmen were outraged at the attack on their way of life, and they looked for some way to ignore it.

In the Senate, members simply agreed informally to table every antislavery petition that was introduced. The House of Representatives, however, decided to institute a formal "gag rule" designed to prevent discussion of antislavery petitions. The first such attempt was made by South Carolina representative James Hammond on December 18, 1835 when he moved that the House refuse to receive such petitions.

The House decided on a policy that would not only prohibit debate, but would also prevent any written record of the receipt of antislavery petitions. On May 26, 1836, by a vote of 117 to 68, the House passed the following resolution:

> "That all petitions... relating in any way, or to any extent whatever, to the subject of slavery, or the abolition of slavery, shall without being either printed or referred, be laid upon the table, and that no further action whatever shall be had thereon."

Thus, the political coalition of proslavery forces in Congress known as the "Slave Power" blocked the Constitutional right of United States citizens to petition their government. Legislators viewed petitions as requests rather than efforts at political lobbying, and they knew that ignoring them would not affect the outcome of any election because women could not vote anyway.

A New York editor sneered that women "had better be shaking *bed-ticks* rather than *poli-tics*." The gag rule was strengthened and renewed each year, and it remained in effect until it was rescinded on Dec. 2, 1844. The importance of the gag rule was that although it silenced the political efforts of women, it acted as a recruiting tool for the abolitionist movement by angering so many people over the intentional squelching of free speech.[48]

One other antislavery activity in which women participated was the home-based boycott of the products of slave labor. This was usually a difficult goal because the economy of the entire country was so complexly linked to cheap slave labor. The four major products produced by slavery were cotton, sugar, rice and tobacco. Steering clear of slave-produced cotton and sugar required sacrifice and creativity, and because women did most of the sewing and cooking, they were challenged to find alternate sources.

The idea behind the boycott, of course, was that without markets for slave-produced products, the southern plantation system would wither away. Although the boycott achieved little success, some abolitionist families did enthusiastically support it. The Gerrit Smith family was one. They saw it as "our duty" to abstain from the use of such products, even when away from home. Gerrit even suggested trying to make the boycott international, but he eventually gave up the effort when the AASS failed to endorse it.[49]

The antislavery work of women resulted in popularizing the movement as a whole and in aiding their own personal statuses. Women became more visible and more highly educated. They developed organizational and public speaking skills necessary for active citizenship in a democracy. They received group therapy benefits that helped to armor them against a male-dominated culture. Their antislavery experience was an initiation for future battles for equality and suffrage. Although one might think that an equity-based culture would encourage such accomplishments, the reaction of the entrenched male leadership was quite to the contrary.[50]

In 1836, Angelina Grimké published the antislavery pamphlet "An Appeal to the Christian Women of the Southern States." It was seized and burned in Charleston, SC and in New Orleans, and Angelina was warned by the Mayor of Charleston never to return to her home state of South Carolina. This was not a southern reaction only; as the Grimké sisters gained notoriety for their public speaking, the Congregational Church of Massachusetts issued a pastoral letter declaring:

> "The power of woman is in her dependence [on men],
> flowing from the consciousness of that weakness which
> God has given her..."[51]

As women's activism shifted from abolition to suffrage after 1840, men often worried that this new focus would dilute the antislavery effort. Abolitionist Elizur Wright feared that the participation of women in human rights issues would "belittle us." He added that "the tom turkeys ought to do the gobbling...." Such bigotry was common in many men.

Even Gerrit Smith exhibited some chauvinism in advocating that women postpone their own goal of suffrage. "Very desirous am I," he wrote, "that justice be done to woman.... But my first duty is to my colored brothers and sisters." Later he would write, "The removal of the political disabilities of race is my first desire, of sex, my second."[52]

Wendell Phillips also wanted women to postpone their suffrage goal, and when men like Phillips and Smith did speak in favor of having women vote, it was usually connected to their desire to pass temperance legislation. The irony in such positions was easy to see; with so much agitation for human rights going on in the antislavery movement, why was it not transferring to the women's rights issue? At the women's rights convention at Akron, Ohio in 1851, Sojourner Truth commented,

> "Where there is so much racket there must be something
> out of kilter. I think that between the niggers of the
> South and the women at the North all talking about
> rights, the white men will be in a fix pretty soon."[53]

In the end, men gave women faint praise. Perhaps men were worried over the increasing political influence of women, or over the possible loss of their own domestic and political superiority. Whatever the reasons, women faced much opposition to their efforts to advance, but they still contributed mightily and sincerely to the antislavery movement. In doing so, they found themselves caught in the social web of opposition to enlightened ideas. And as the moral suasion process moved on, abolitionists confronted both verbal and physical forms of violence from pro-slavery interests.

When the newly built Pennsylvania Hall was first opened in Philadelphia on May 14, 1838, it was hailed as a "Temple of Freedom"—a building to be used as a forum for open discussion of issues regarding human rights. The move to construct the building began in 1836 by reformers in Philadelphia as a reaction to racist actions against blacks that had closed all other buildings to their use. The new Pennsylvania Hall Association that included Quakers James and Lucretia Coffin Mott as board members raised $40,000 by selling stock shares at $20 each.

The auditorium in Pennsylvania Hall held 3,000 people on May 15, 1838 when the American Convention of Anti-Slavery Women held its meeting there, agreeing on resolutions to end slavery in Washington, D.C. and to boycott the products of slave labor. On May 16 the Pennsylvania Anti-Slavery Society held a meeting there, followed by an evening meeting of women antislavery activists. It was at that meeting that Angelina Grimké and Abby Kelley spoke, thereby inflaming a mob that had gathered outside. After more meetings on May 17, black and white women left the hall arm in arm. That night, a racist mob burned Pennsylvania Hall to the ground.

A subsequent investigation committee reported that the speakers were responsible for the fire by having enraged the public.[54]

This happened in the "cradle of freedom" in the supposedly antislavery North. Obviously, abolitionists had enemies there who saw the abolition of slavery as a threat to their elite status. Abolitionists were labeled as "a miserable clique of fanatics," "pestilent incendiaries," "negro stealers," or "amalgamators" by an aristocracy who feared that the democratic principles of majority rule and free speech could undermine their power and influence.[55]

The new antislavery organizations of the early 1830s successfully appealed to the masses at the 'grass-roots' level for support, thus bypassing and undermining the older elite power brokers. Old and established patterns of influence and decision-making were being threatened; leaders were becoming followers; gentlemen were becoming commoners; and, worst of all, blacks were becoming respected citizens.

As these traditional patterns of deference changed, white leaders began to see themselves as an "aggrieved class" that felt they were victims of a conspiracy against their privileged status. The result was that these "gentlemen of property and standing" became terrorists fighting against the incoming tide of human rights issues. As moral suasionists attempted to guide the public attitude in favor of abolition, vested interests in the status quo fought back.[56]

Pro-slavery interests denounced abolitionists as fanatics and idealists who were creating radicals bent on destroying society by instigating slave conspiracies and insurrections. Paranoia ruled as they accused abolitionists of social crimes that threatened national stability.

They feared the growing power of the antislavery movement as it spread from Boston into New York City and upstate New York where liberal philanthropists like the Tappan brothers and Gerrit Smith fueled it with profits from successful businesses. As the number of new antislavery organizations increased, so did the intensity and frequency of violent responses.[57]

After 1834, the public backlash against abolition included censoring antislavery mail sent into the South, opposition to and destruction of schools designed to educate blacks, hanging abolitionists in effigy with notes attached that were signed by "Judge Lynch," and the delivery of proslavery speeches in the national legislature. President Andrew Jackson famously declared antislavery literature to be "wicked."[58]

The pro-slavery tactics were expressions of terrorism. They stoned speakers, burned buildings, dragged leaders through the streets, tarred and feathered them, murdered them, and threatened their livelihoods and families. Garrison called it a "reign of terror." By far the most visible of the proslavery terrorist tactics was the mob.[59]

Mobs led by upstanding citizens attacked antislavery individuals and meetings as a common feature of northern life in the latter half of the 1830s. The mob was viewed as a legitimate response to the threat posed by abolitionists to the racial status quo. They represented a white response to black attempts at freedom, and elite white support for it. Actually, the mobs, gag rules, and other forms of violence against abolitionists exposed the depravity of the proslavery cause. Some abolitionists viewed mob violence against them as a sign of their success, with the pro-slavery mobs representing the death throes of a receding ideal.

Those abolitionists who spoke in public in northern cities were frequently mobbed. Henry B. Stanton and Theodore D. Weld were each mobbed over 100 times. Weld once commented,

> "The Mayor and the City Officers [of Pawtucket, Rhode Island] were with a few exceptions totally inefficient, and pursued such a course to embolden rather than to intimidate the mob.... Stones, pieces of bricks, eggs, cents, sticks... were thrown at me while speaking.... I... was hit by two stones, tho' not hurt seriously."[60]

The Smithfield Presbyterian Church, site of the first meeting of the New York State Anti-Slavery Society on October 22, 1835.

From the author's collection

Gerrit Smith first experienced the impact of an anti-abolition mob on October 21, 1835 in Utica, New York. As a spectator attending a meeting to establish the New York State Anti-Slavery Society, he watched a mob of local business and political leaders disrupt the meeting and demand its immediate dissolution. Concerned over the disruption of free speech, Smith invited those attending to reassemble at Peterboro on the following day to continue their proceedings. Over 300 persons did so, traveling the 30 miles to Peterboro on a rainy, cold night. On October 22, they reconvened in the local Presbyterian Church for the first full meeting of the new organization.

Smith himself was also mobbed on several occasions during public speeches. On one occasion in Ithaca, NY, the following poster announced his scheduled appearance:

"Down with abolition
Fellow citizens, A foul abolitionist; a
'Child of the Devil', will hold forth
today at the Presbyterian Church,
at 11 o'clock. Let every good
citizen attend to KEEP ORDER. April 27"

Smith annotated his personal copy: "Many copies of this were stuck up in Ithaca the morning of the day I spoke there in Apl 1839."[61]

Mob participants usually rationalized their action by claiming that abolitionist activity threatened northern commerce linked to southern trade, or that abolitionists were "amalgamationists" who advocated racial intermarriage. They also blamed the abolitionists for instigating the violence by intentionally stirring up the passions of the masses. As late as 1861, a mob in Syracuse, NY broke up an antislavery convention attended by Gerrit Smith, Samuel J. May, Beriah Green, Susan B. Anthony and others. May later recalled that the mob burned their effigies in the streets "amid shouts, hootings, mingled with disgusting profanity and ribaldry."[62]

Specific pro-slavery actions like mob violence emanated from a general but latent northern attitude that supported slavery. A union existed between slave owners in the South and property and business owners in the North. Northern bankers, manufacturers, and

The building that housed the Church of Peterboro founded by Gerrit Smith still stands on the southeast corner of the square in Peterboro.

From the author's collection

shippers had developed a high and vested interest in maintaining slavery because it was so profitable to them. Their morality was easily overwhelmed by greed. As Wendell Phillips put it, in a capitalist economy, "Mr. Cash is a more efficient master than Mr. Lash."

Northern businessmen feared that war or disunion would cause them to lose trade and would allow southern debtors who owed them over $300 million to default. As late as 1862, Horatio Seymour was elected to the New York State governorship as an anti-emancipation candidate because of the public fear that black freedom would destroy the northern economy. In 1861 Fernando Wood, a former congressman and mayor of New York City, proposed that the city secede along with the southern states in order to maintain partnership with the geographical area that supported its businesses. Northern corporate complicity with slavery was seen in support for ship building, lumber and dock workers, and in financing and insurance connections with southern plantations.[63]

Northern violence against abolitionists found many expressions. Garrison was threatened with arrest for libel, and he often hid in

other abolitionists' homes for protection. Destruction of abolitionists' homes and other property terrorized them. When the office of
publisher and former slave owner James G. Birney was destroyed in
1836, he remarked,

> "What strange times we are fallen on to be sure! That in
> the state of Ohio, a man who has been brought up in the
> midst of slavery, and professes to know its evils, should be
> threatened with degrading inflictions, cruel whippings
> and death, for speaking and writing about them."

The next year in Alton, Illinois, publisher Elijah Lovejoy was
murdered for printing antislavery material.[64]

One major institution throughout the nation that supported
slavery was the Christian Church. Abolitionists agreed so completely on this that they often dropped out of established Christian denominations to form their own antislavery church. The
Free Church, as it was usually called to emphasize its freedom
from sectarian doctrine, blossomed in the North. In January of
1839, the non-sectarian and abolition-oriented Evangelical Union
Anti-Slavery Society was formed with Birney as its president. Gerrit
Smith left the Smithfield Presbyterian Church in 1843 to form the
Church of Peterboro—a political forum for the abolitionist Liberty
Party. He said of the established churches,

> "the Church, comprising no very small portion of the
> whole population, and exerting a mighty influence for
> good or ill on the residue, is tainted, yes, rotten with
> slavery."

Smith abhorred the "Union-saving and slave-catching sermons
of devil-deluded and devil-driven Doctors of Divinity."

Abolitionist Stephen Foster angrily called the Christian
churches "combinations of thieves, robbers, adulterers, pirates, and

murderers, and, as such... the bulwark of American slavery."

Even the less radical Samuel J. May accused the churches and clergy of being guilty of prolonging slavery. "The most outrageous mobs we encountered," he said, "were led on or instigated by persons professing to be religious."

Church leaders generally saw human intervention to abolish slavery as unnecessary, because God would eventually do it when He saw fit. Garrison detested this view:

> "The blood of souls is upon [the church's] garments, yet she heeds not the stain. The clankings of the prisoner's chains strike upon her ear, but they cannot penetrate her heart."[65]

The obvious ingredient in American life that caused such opposition to the abolition of slavery was racism. By the 1830s, violence had already occurred against black communities in northern cities. The antislavery movement did not cause the negrophobia evident in mobs and churches, but it gave it expression. While most abolitionists themselves possessed a trace of racist thought as measured by today's standards, it is to their credit that they were able to control its expression and effects. Northern racism served as a prop for slavery—even as moral and economic rationales for its existence evaporated.[66]

Antislavery northerners were largely content with ineffective schemes such as "gradual abolition," the non-extension of slavery into new territories, or even colonization, as long as blacks did not encroach on their own privileges. Most did not actually like the idea of slavery, but they feared emancipation. As Thomas Jefferson put it, having slavery in existence was like holding a wolf by the ears—you didn't like it, but didn't dare let go.

As if opposition to abolition were not intense enough in the North, in the South it was simply brutal. I have described the physical brutality of slavery in detail in other works. The brutality against the slave's mind is of equal significance.[67]

Southern author and apologist for slavery George Fitzhugh—a cousin of Ann Carroll Fitzhugh Smith, Gerrit's wife—wrote two books in the 1850s in support of slavery. He defended the institution at a biological level, claiming that blacks were naturally inferior to whites. His claim was that

> "men are not born physically, morally or intellectually equal.... Their natural inequalities beget inequalities of rights.... It would be far nearer the truth to say, 'that some were born with saddles on their backs, and others booted and spurred to ride them,'—and the riding does them good."

He focused on differences between people rather than the similarities among all humans: "Subordination, difference of caste and classes, difference of sex, age and slavery beget peace and good will."

Such a biased view of human ability by people with the power to rule made the definition of the inferior black person a self-fulfilling prophecy. Fitzhugh took the indictment a step further by claiming that "the unrestricted exploitation [of free blacks by] free society is more oppressive to the laborer than domestic slavery."[68]

This fantasy world of southern thought justified abuse of all types, and it led major institutions to develop a culture of hate. Interestingly, at about the same time that Fitzhugh was publishing his ideas in 1857, Charles Darwin's work on natural selection was proving the fallacy behind the idea that skin color rendered humans fundamentally different. Darwin had become disgusted during his Edinburgh University days in the mid-1820s with the use of the pseudo-science of phrenology to support the lie of black inferiority. He developed a passion for discovering facts about human evolution. Slavery to him was "that monstrous stain on our boasted liberty...." He saw phrenology as static pessimism regarding the chances for social reform, and evolutionism as an agent of change.

Darwin's ideas about the common origin of life and the "unity of man" broke forth as civil war was erupting in the United States. Those ideas helped set the stage for the epic clash of white superiority versus democratic equality.

If black labor was essential to the southern economy, and the economy was not doing well, blacks could be blamed. And if whites had to help do menial work, then the culture could not advance. The vicious cycle of cause and effect kept blacks mentally and physically under the lash, and in a position of representing political and economic power for whites who were not about to be persuaded to give up the reins.[69]

Perhaps the epitome of the abuse of slaves was viewed through what northerners called the "Slave Power." That term referred to the domination of social institutions—especially political institutions—by southern states. The fact that the Constitution allowed slave states to count three-fifths of their resident slaves as part of a representable population added to their control of votes taken in the national legislature and the electoral college.

In 1820 this amounted to twenty additional representatives in Congress, and it gave southern states the power to elect pro-slavery presidents. In fact, if the three-fifths rule had not influenced Congressional votes, Missouri would not have become a slave state in 1820, new territory acquired after the Mexican War would have been free, and neither the Kansas-Nebraska Act nor the House's "gag rule" would have been passed. Property in slaves had become the legal basis for some representation, and northerners claimed that their horses and cows should be so counted.[70]

Besides the House's gag rule regarding the discussion of public petitions, evidence of the success of the Slave Power included churches being goaded into a state of moral paralysis, mob violence being blamed on victims, the fact that both houses of the national legislature proposed Constitutional amendments to prevent the abolition of slavery, and the threatening of citizens for simply possessing antislavery literature.[71]

In some southern states it was illegal to possess a copy of *Uncle Tom's Cabin*. In Charleston, SC in 1835 a mob broke into a post office and confiscated and burned American Anti-Slavery Society pamphlets. In Nashville, Tennessee, former Lane rebel Amos Dresser was publicly whipped for possessing such pamphlets, and miles away from the capitol, in Georgetown, Dr. Ruben Crandall (brother of educator Prudence Crandall) was jailed for possession of an American Anti-Slavery Society newspaper. As the paranoia of southern slave owners spread, so also did resistance to abuse among slaves—and the determination of antislavery forces to succeed.[72]

By the mid-1830s, abolitionists viewed southern institutions that supported slavery as a threat to their own liberty. Gerrit Smith proclaimed that northerners must oppose slavery in self-defense lest they become enslaved to immoral southern ideas. By 1808 when the foreign slave trade legally ended, every northern state had abolished slavery. None of the southern states had done so, and three decades later, the same situation existed. Abolitionists who had invested all resources at their command in the process of moral suasion were becoming convinced that it was a failed tactic.[73]

Long-term efforts at moral suasion had yielded nothing except more new slave states and half a million more slaves. Wendell Phillips admitted that after "twenty years of incessant strife... the treasury is empty, the hand is tired, the toil of many years has gained but little...."[74]

An important principle to understand at the outset of any critique of moral suasion is that the moral suasionists were *right*—and they still are. As Garrison knew, to abolish slavery by law "would be useless without transformation of the spirit that the law reflected." That is, changing laws is easy; changing minds is not. The irony of abolitionism is that a movement cannot succeed just by being *right*. The optimism of the early moral suasionists was founded in the faulty premises that northerners were not racist, and that southerners would listen to moral messages. But as frustration developed, hard-working abolitionists like Gerrit Smith found pro-slavery persons to be "impatient of contradiction, self-willed, supercilious, cruel, [and] devilish...."[75]

In part, the fault of the moral suasionists was their focus on individual reform rather than the struggle for institutional power. Although this approach was true to the nineteenth-century model of reform—to reform oneself first and trust that the example will transfer to others—it ignored the developing centralization of power that was beginning to characterize the new capitalist society.

As passionate social agitators who had seen the light of future perfection for society, the abolitionists felt certain of success as soon as they could get the rest of their seemingly enlightened fellows to follow suit. But the riotous and repressive nature of white northern response to immediatism surprised them and retarded their visions of quick gains. Reactionaries called the abolitionists "fanatical crusaders," "incendiaries," "cold-hearted, base and malignant libelers," "instigators," and "ignorant, infatuated barbarians." Such reactions actually stimulated interest in them and in their work, and acted as a recruiting tool as more northerners added their sympathies to the movement.[76]

These "crusaders" became more aware of the defeatist power of the vicious circle of slavery and prejudice. As they felt the dead weight of cultural inertia, they realized that moral suasion was ineffective as a technique for pursuing change. Theodore Weld highlighted the depth of the prejudice he saw in a letter to New York City businessman and abolitionist Lewis Tappan, noting that such reform activity might rustle the leaves of the tree, but left "branches, trunk, and deep shot roots, to propagate anew with a vigor of production vastly increased by the pruning." The search for alternatives to moral suasion led some of the abolitionists to seriously consider political activity.[77]

In his speech at the 1836 annual meeting of the American Anti-Slavery Society, Gerrit Smith planted the seeds for changing the focus of abolitionists from moral conversion of the South to the social defense of the North. Northerners, he warned, should pay more attention to protecting their own rights than trying to change the attitudes of southerners. Politics would be their vehicle.

Even Wendell Phillips, a Garrisonian, agreed that abolitionists had become "weary of this moral suasion, and sigh for something tangible, some power they can feel." Although Phillips would not become very supportive, he at least saw tactics other than moral suasion as legitimate ways to attack biased institutions.[78]

One of those tactics was to encourage civic engagement on the part of the masses. This was a practical rather than a moral approach, involving more voting than preaching. The idea appealed to practical thinkers like Gerrit Smith, James G. Birney, and others who were "westerners" from New York State or Ohio and not part of the Boston-centered "suasionist clique." Birney was influential in harnessing Smith's practicality, saying "that repentance [of the slave owner] is far off, if at all to be expected."[79]

Because both major political parties—Democrats and Whigs—maintained a code of silence regarding slavery in an effort to acquire a coalition of votes, Birney and Smith began to discuss the possibility of creating a third party with a focus on the abolition of slavery. This suggestion, of course, worried the moral suasionists.

Lydia Maria Child opposed the formation of a third party be-

cause she felt it would sap energy and might never elect more than a
few antislavery legislators.

> "I too want to see all our legislators anti-slavery; but
> when that time comes, there will most obviously be no
> need for a distinct abolition party; and in order to bring
> about that time, we must diligently exert moral influence
> to sway *all* parties...."

Child foresaw hypocrisy in political rather than moral change,
and she warned that the original cause of the oppression would
remain.

New Hampshire abolitionist Nathaniel P. Rogers stated the
concern most clearly: "The best... that political movements... could
effect for the slave, is to translate him into... a 'free nigger.'"[80]

Moral suasionists wanted to build a constituency that favored
the equal treatment of all people as a humane goal; political advocates wanted to force that goal on an unwilling public. But the
public seemed to be becoming more frustrated with moral suasion
by the end of the 1830s, and many people were at least willing to
listen to the politicians.

It would take another two decades before Garrison saw the
logic in supporting political activity. In 1856, he announced that
those who must vote should support the new Republican Party's
candidate John C. Fremont. By the start of the Civil War four years
later, he had agreed that political gains achieved through war were
better than wasting more time waiting for moral suasion to work.
Antislavery activist and editor Jane Swisshelm wondered in her
1880 autobiography "whether [Garrison had] labored harder for
the overthrow of slavery or political anti-slavery."[81]

But as 1840 approached, political solutions were gaining support, and the tide turned.

~ 6 ~

Politics

Antislavery voter success "would be the knocking of a stone out of the arch of American slavery...."
- Gerrit Smith, 1843

While William Lloyd Garrison's ideas about moral suasion were right in the long term, Gerrit Smith's ideas about politics were right in the short term. To the practical Smith, moral change would take many decades, but political change could happen quickly.

Smith viewed political activity as the logical consequence of efforts at moral suasion. "Moral suasion," he said, "is... indispensable to the antislavery cause: but it is so, mainly because of the political action which is its legitimate result."

Decades later, as an old man, Smith would repeat the thought: "Political action... is resorted to in order to carry out and make effective our moral influence." Smith felt that those who would not or could not do whatever it took, and change tactics as the movement matured, were mired in stagnation.

Garrison knew that "The politics of a people will always be shaped by its morals, as the vane on the steeple is ever indicating in what direction the wind blows." He wanted the moral wind to blow first in a nondiscriminatory direction so that the decision to abolish slavery would reflect willing change. He regarded the "political people" not as moral philosophers, but as impatient social agitators who were selfishly forcing premature changes in laws upon an as-yet unwilling public. To Garrison, political victory would be a repudiation of the necessity of a moral revolution.[1]

It is likely that most abolitionists shared Garrison's wish for moral suasion, but frustration drove them to try alternatives. Former President John Quincy Adams expressed his frustration with moral suasion to Gerrit Smith, calling it the "loss of a cherished hope."[2]

Smith chose politics as the way to achieve abolition, but he made the choice with serious doubts. First, he knew that moral attitude change was necessary if new laws were to have the desired affect. Second, he thought of the political process as an unprincipled attempt to please everyone. He felt that politicians would dilute the moral quality of abolitionism, as they placed a higher priority on elective office than on principled goals.

"Politicians" he wrote, "are apt to die poor—especially such of them as espouse principle." Third, Smith was not a politician and had no ambition to become one. "It will be long," he claimed, "before I consent to be, and very long, before I ask to be a candidate for civil office...."[3]

Smith's choice of supporting political activity was purely practical. He liked to see the results of his work and his philanthropy in quickly visible or tangible forms. Voting results had provided such evidence; they could be displayed as an example of what could be achieved, and they were useful in showing other communities an example of successful reform. At the same time, Smith was optimistic about the ability of the public to vote rationally, once it had read or listened to well-reasoned appeals. He warned northerners that they would someday have reason for remorse if they were "not willing to vote slavery out of existence." [4]

Garrison's anti-governmental stance, his non-resistance tactics, and his refusal to vote appeared to Smith to be a denial of the power of existing institutions to effect change. It did not credit citizens—black or white—with the ability to foster their own goals of freedom. When the Massachusetts Anti-Slavery Society met in January of 1839, Henry B. Stanton and James G. Birney pressed the issue of choosing to support either moral suasion or political action. Although the society chose to support neither, the battle over preferred tactics had become polarized, and the stage was set for the antislavery movement to split into factions.[5]

The cultural era of the late 1830s encouraged political activity based in factions. The economic depression that hit in 1837 destabilized white society and upset traditional patterns of power. Blacks began to emerge as more powerful social actors through new organizations, conventions, political activity, and the publication of alternative newspapers. They became more willing to express themselves and to fight against the degradations they had faced as slaves or as lower class citizens. The "panic"—as the depression was called—altered old perceptions and expectations and touched off serious efforts to reform social institutions.[6]

In the North, optimism inspired by the revival spirit of the Second Great Awakening fused an emphasis on moral conscience with the emerging interest in practical politics. The South did not experience such cultural stimulation, remaining stagnant with people and institutions mired in an anachronistic effort to maintain honor through white supremacy. The result was a divergence of politics, with the North becoming more liberal and the South more conservative.

The ensuing decades of the 1840s and 1850s produced a brand of politics in which the political parties were more important than the politicians. The political contests at the national level were not just between rival party members who shook hands later; they were symptoms of a deep-seated moral struggle in which aspects of slavery and liberty confronted one another.

Political parties were sectional and were defined by subcultural biases and prejudices. Being a member of a party carried as much identity and constriction with it as did being a member of a church. The mechanisms of politics were driven by party ideology, not by popular or powerful individuals with particular personalities. Candidates were not the drawing cards for attracting votes; party mandates and beliefs were. Even the presidents of the era were dull, unknown standard-bearers—Harrison, Tyler (elected as vice president), Polk, Taylor, Fillmore (elected as vice president), Pierce, Buchanan, and even Lincoln. It was the party that was elected more than the man.[7]

The antislavery parties that developed during the era also fit this mold. The Liberty Party, the Liberty League/Radical Abolition Party, the Free Soil Party, the Free Democrat Party, and eventually, the Republican Party fielded lackluster candidates behind all-important ideals. Gerrit Smith never identified with a major political party, and when he finally entered the field of political competition reluctantly, he did so as an abolition candidate.

In general, abolitionists were either apolitical or did not quite know where to set their roots. There was no precedent for antislavery political activity until 1840, so those interested in supporting political activity landed with whatever new party emerged. The internal splits within the parties created shifting loyalties. As Reform-Era researcher and author Eric Foner has noted, "Party loyalty... was not the radicals' forté."[8]

A major force that led some abolitionists toward political activity was the domination of national institutions by pro-slavery interests—The Slave Power. Freedom of speech and assembly by antislavery groups were often threatened or physically endangered by mobs in the late 1830s. Major political parties pandered to pro-slavery interests by appealing for votes through white voters' racial prejudices. Journalist Elijah Lovejoy's murder, the burning of Pennsylvania Hall, and the confiscation of antislavery mail all pointed to increasing opposition to abolition by powerful forces. In several letters to abolitionist colleagues, Gerrit Smith lamented the Slave Power and hoped that a new antislavery political effort would be able to undermine it.[9]

Throughout the 1830s and 1840s, the two major national political parties—Democratic and Whig—catered to pro-slavery interests so consistently that abolitionist observers came to recognize the need for their own party. Massachusetts senator Charles Sumner noted, "The pro-slavery party, controlling every branch of the government, was able to make, to execute, and to interpret laws. It wielded the whole patronage of the nation...." He noted, "It will not be the first time in history that the hosts of slavery have outnumbered the champions of freedom."[10]

Gerrit Smith chastised Whig Party member William Seward:
> "It is in the light of this... proslavery character of our National parties, that I see how baseless and vain are your hopes of good from the Whig party."

To his neighbors in Madison County, Smith warned,
> "How vain for you to hope, that parties which hold the poor black man in slavery, will be true to the poor white man."[11]

Politicians in both parties generally did not perceive the danger involved in the antagonism between liberty and slavery as early as did the abolitionists. Men like James G. Birney and Gerrit Smith saw the probability of war as early as the mid-1840s, whereas the politicians believed that they could quell the fires of controversy with compromise. Transcendentalist Ralph Waldo Emerson in

his "Lecture on Slavery" spoke of "an era when governors do not
govern, when judges do not judge, when Presidents do not preside,
and when representatives do not represent." He was referring to the
timidity of Democratic leaders in the face of the Slave Power; he
claimed that they ignored natural law. His quip "Cotton thread
holds the Union together" drew attention to the mercenary alli-
ance between the textile businesses of the North and the cotton
produced by slave labor in the South. Such a linkage, he claimed,
supported the pro-slavery stance of political parties.[12]

Charles Sumner stated well the case for antislavery politics:

> "At the present time in our country there exists a deep,
> controlling, conscientious feeling against slavery.... If
> not *through* the old parties then *over* the old parties
> this irresistible current *shall* find its way. It cannot be
> permanently stopped. If the old parties will not become
> its organs they must become its victims. The party of
> freedom will certainly prevail."[13]

The party that emerged to fill this role was the Liberty Party.
The first serious action taken to form an independent antislavery
political party occurred in an Oswego County convention on October 4, 1839 when abolitionists nominated a third-party ticket of
local candidates for the state legislature.

This was followed on Nov. 13 and 14, 1839 by a nominating
convention in Warsaw, New York where James G. Birney and Francis Julius LeMoyne were nominated for president and vice president.
Both later declined. A subsequent convention was held in Arcade,
NY on Jan. 28 and 29, 1840 to decide what to do next. Over 500
men attended, led by Myron Holley and Gerrit Smith. They issued
a call for a nominating convention to be held in Albany, NY on
April 1, 1840.

The apolitical Garrison called them "April fools."[14]

Before the Albany convention met, antislavery political leaders James G. Birney, William Goodell and Gerrit Smith met in February "around the fire in the Smith home in Peterboro" to discuss the pending new party. Smith suggested that it be called the "Liberty Party" in recognition of its fundamental differences with the ideas of the two major parties.[15]

The Albany convention was billed as "The National Convention of Friends of Immediate Emancipation." Chaired by Utica lawyer Alvan Stewart, it drew noted abolitionists from most New England states as well as from the "western" states of New York and Ohio. James G. Birney and Thomas Earle accepted their respective nominations for president and vice president, but did little campaigning. Party leaders did not expect to win elections. They wanted to shake up the status quo, perhaps control the balance of power between the two major parties, and place their antislavery issues and message before the public.

It is important to note that this early stage of political activity laid the foundation for the political movement that would capture the presidency in 1860. Gerrit Smith foresaw that development by noting that those antislavery people who were more moderate than the radical abolitionist Liberty Party, and more "principled" than the Democratic or Whig parties, would be likely to form a new party in between these others.[16]

The Liberty Party was molded in large part by the tenets of Gerrit Smith. He believed in the early 1840s that political action could end slavery without war, and he saw the Liberty Party as an attempt to secularize the cause of abolition without losing its moral purpose. Alienating moralists like Garrison and "religionists" like Lewis Tappan, he maintained the moral endeavor by connecting the political efforts of the party to the Free-Church movement.

Smith called the Liberty Party "a religious party" based on principles of human rights. He opened the Free-Church pulpit as a forum for speakers with messages that reflected the party's goal of creating "righteous civil government." Liberty Party members were proud of saying that they lived, spoke, and preached human rights ideas as political evangelicals. They referred to their "conversion experience" as acceptance of the need for immediate abolition. Their focus on human rights grew out of the significance they placed on "natural law."

William Blackstone, in his "Commentaries on the Laws of England," (1765) had prioritized natural law or God's law over "positive law" established by people, and abolitionists generally accepted this distinction as their rationale for abolishing slavery. As an example of its application, Gerrit Smith once wrote about a court case in which the owner of a fugitive slave had asked a judge what better evidence could be required of ownership of the slave than the original Bill of Sale. The judge replied, "A Bill of Sale from God Almighty."[19]

The Liberty Party members' faith in the possibility of a political solution to slavery grew in part out of having watched the success of antislavery organizations during the 1830s. The fact that hundreds of thousands of people had joined antislavery societies and had become informed about the injustices of slavery gave them reason to be optimistic about change. It appeared that the new network of antislavery interests would be a voting base for Liberty Party candidates, and that many would believe, as Smith did, that

> "As one who subscribes to the fundamental doctrine of a Republic that 'all men are created equal'—I [have] no right to cast a vote for any person but [one who believes likewise]..."[20]

When it came to actually acquiring votes, the Liberty Party was not very successful. Its one-issue platform was weak in the face of national economic issues that arose with the Panic of 1837. Although they did implicate their stands on issues that they believed to be controlled by the Slave Power, Liberal Party candidates did not pursue them directly, and their appeal was limited to voters interested in abolition.

In Smith's home territory, the Liberty Party did garner more votes than elsewhere. Between 1842 and 1847, only 14.4 percent of Madison County voters favored Liberty Party candidates; in Smith's own Town of Smithfield, that number was just 44.3 percent. This modest number spoke to the local popularity and influence of Smith, but on the larger scale, the party's influence was small. Even some abolitionists did not vote for Liberty Party candidates, thereby prompting claims of hypocrisy.[21]

By 1847, some of the politically oriented abolitionists had become so dissatisfied with the low public appeal of the Liberty Party that they advocated expansion of its platform to include many issues besides the abolition of slavery. They met June 8 through 10, 1847 at Macedon Lock, NY to discuss the issues to be addressed in an expanded platform. The meeting led them to split off from the Liberty Party to form the Liberty League. They nominated Gerrit Smith for president.[22]

This new expanded-issue initiative for Smith was another illustration of his practical approach to success. Having perceived the realities of public opinion, he altered his course in a way designed to garner support for the antislavery movement. Holding on to the one issue stand of the Liberty Party, he maintained, would assure the loss of a support base for liberal ideas once the issue of slavery was resolved.

Other practical-thinking abolitionists like Frederick Douglass, William Goodell, and James G. Birney supported Smith in this endeavor to make their long-term goals possible. The moral suasion group, however, reacted negatively. Garrison publicly vilified Douglass for moving to Rochester, NY, starting his own newspaper, and supporting the political movement.[23]

Before we trace the party effort further, it is important to address an important aspect of the advent of political antislavery activity that caused an internal split in the antislavery movement.

By the late 1830s, as moral suasion came to be seen by more practical abolitionists as an ineffective technique, Garrison was losing influence. In some ways, he even seemed like a pro-slavery person: He advocated disunion as a way of escaping the effects of what be believed to be a pro-slavery United States Constitution. He saw the Bible (which most people loved) as a pro-slavery document. And he opposed political action, the very technique that had been built into the new republic as the way to pursue orderly institutional change.

Garrison had become a tragic figure in the movement against slavery. Although he was right in his 'moral-suasion-first' stand, he could not see that the intensity of racial prejudice throughout the nation would not allow moral suasion to work.

Determined to maintain a dominant position of leadership in the antislavery movement, Garrison gained control of the American Anti-Slavery Society at its 1840 New York City convention by stacking the voting attendees with 464 friendly delegates from his home state of Massachusetts. Although this move worked for him, the irony is that those politically oriented abolitionists in attendance cared little; they had already established an alternative organization and power base in the Liberty Party. With its use of the Free Church as a forum for speakers advocating particular public policy changes, the Liberty Party had taken on the role of an antislavery society.[24]

About 300 members of the 1840 convention withdrew following the stacked vote, and formed what amounted to an affiliate of the Liberty Party: the American and Foreign Anti-Slavery Society. Its leaders were the same men who had been influential in establishing the Liberty Party: Gerrit Smith, Joshua Leavitt, John Greenleaf Whittier. Their philosophical purpose was to discredit the Garrisonians' claim that the American national government was too repressive and was unconcerned with the abolition of slavery. They also wished to restore the respectability of abolitionism.[25]

Their approach to these goals was to wean northern voters from their allegiance to the pro-slavery Whig and Democrat Parties and to recruit them for the Liberty Party. The most fertile area for such work was in the "burned-over district" of New York State, western Massachusetts, and the "western reserve" in Ohio. By 1840, the significance of skin color in American thought had become clear to these politically oriented abolitionists, and the issues they now faced were pan-cultural: racial integration vs. black separatism; civil disobedience vs. political violence; racial bias vs. social justice.[26]

As practical politicians, their tactics were designed to patch up a corrupt system, not to morally change a corrupt society. Their technique of merging dreams with practical reality left them susceptible to the Garrisonians' warning that political success without moral commitment equalled war. Although they knew the risk of potential violence was high, it did not bother them much; they realized that war was probably inevitable anyway.

One of their arguments that demonstrated the practical quality of their thought was the economic one. It was clear to them that the technological advance and prosperity of the North contrasted with the stagnation and depression of the South. Free labor, they claimed, stimulated initiative and growth, whereas slave labor was a disincentive to productivity. They even blamed the Panic of 1837 on southern dependence on slave labor.[27]

Some of the most radical of these political abolitionists were black. Their ability to feel prejudice evidently drew blacks into the political arena as a practical means of achieving success in abolition. During the early 1840s, when the Liberty Party had the political antislavery movement all to itself, the moral message of justice and equality was clear. It compelled northern blacks to endorse James G. Birney as the Liberty Party presidential candidate in 1840 and again in 1844.

Henry Highland Garnet, William Wells Brown, Frederick Douglass, Jermain Wesley Loguen, James W. Pennington, Samuel Ringgold Ward, James McCune Smith—all were attracted to the practical techniques of abolition work. McCune Smith and Douglass became closely involved with powerful white men like Gerrit Smith and John Brown in business deals designed to aid the social status of blacks, including land distribution and newspaper publishing.[28]

The mid-1840s was a critical time period for attracting abolitionists into the political arena. President Polk engaged the military in a "pre-emptive strike" against Mexico to gain more territory for the extension of slavery. This angered many who then joined the abolition crusade. Douglass moved from Boston to Rochester in 1847 to escape Garrison's influence and to be free to start his own newspaper. Smith met Brown in 1848 and began to consider more active—and perhaps even violent—ways of pursuing abolition. And as previously noted, the political abolitionists reinvented the church as a quasi-political institution.

Abolitionist Elizur Wright referred to a "fogland" of Christian theology when it came to abolition. He claimed that ministers were endorsing "prejudice and oppression" as they instructed worshipers "doing their weekly penance to God in cushioned pews."

William Goodell, abolitionist and pastor of an independent antislavery church in Honeoye, NY, coined the term "ecclesiastical abolitionist" to describe the "come-outers" who had abandoned mainline Christian denominations and formed non-sectarian Free Churches allied with political abolitionism. Gerrit Smith helped establish two such churches in Oswego and Peterboro.[29]

A major concern of the Free Church and the political abolition movement as a whole was the protection of free speech. It was Gerrit Smith's focus in his address at the first meeting of the New York State Anti-Slavery Society in Peterboro on October 22, 1835. Free speech came to be used as a vehicle to transform the moral debate over slavery into a political debate. It was the focus of opposition to the Congressional "gag rule" against the open discussion of anti-slavery petitions, and it became the justification for public meetings that involved the discussion of slavery.[30]

With Smith's influence, the Madison County Anti-Slavery Society scheduled 31 "anti-slavery meetings" throughout the county between Sept. 28 and Nov. 2, 1840. It hosted an Abolition/Liberty Party convention in Peterboro in 1842. At that convention, artwork depicted a kneeling slave exclaiming, "Talk for me—Write for me—Print for me—Paint for me—Pray for me—Vote for me."

Both the free-speech and political themes appear here. In an interesting parallel incident, in 1841 New Haven artist Nathaniel Jocelyn had painted a portrait of Cinque—victor in the Amistad mutiny case—that the Philadelphia-based Artist Fund Society refused to display in its annual exhibition. Society representatives explained that it was "contrary to usage to display works of that character, believing that under the [racial] excitement of the times, it might prove injurious to the proprietors and the institution." [31]

The city of Syracuse, just west of Madison County, also supported these political themes; between 1845 and 1850, the city hosted 12 major antislavery conventions and over two dozen other smaller antislavery meetings. Overall, the political antislavery movement garnered consistent support in the "psychic highway" corridor from western Massachusetts through New York and into Ohio. But it would need to form a wider base and more inclusive coalitions before it could become a national political force.[32]

Such a coalition began to form in the mid-1840s. In August 1846, pro-slavery President Polk asked Congress to appropriate money for the purchase of land from Mexico. Antislavery Democrat Congressman David Wilmot (PA) introduced a resolution declaring that such land acquisitions be forever free of slavery. Although the "Wilmot Proviso" never passed into law, it became a model for free-soil opposition to the extension of slavery.[33]

By 1848, the non-extension of slavery theme had attracted the interest of the more conservative wing of the Liberty Party. Antislavery factions from within both the Whig and Democrat parties formed the new Free Soil Party. Gerrit Smith viewed this move as an effort by biased white men to avoid the issue of emancipation of oppressed black people in order to attract votes. Because he could not abandon his commitment to human rights, he opted for allegiance to the more radical Liberty League.

The election of 1848 was a critical turning point in the political antislavery effort. The U.S. had recently acquired land from Mexico, and the question arose whether the new area of Texas should be admitted to the Union as a free or slave state. This focused the attention of both major parties on the issue of the extension of slavery.

The nominating conventions of both the Whig and Democrat parties in 1848 produced clear evidence of growing non-extension factions. The "Barn-burner Democrats" (so named because of their seeming willingness to destroy the party in order to get their own way—like the farmer who burned his barn to rid it of rats) opposed the extension of slavery. So did the "Cotton Whigs," who were, in fact, pro-slavery. Both conventions ignored these non-extension factions and nominated pro-slavery candidates—Taylor (Whig) and Polk (Democrat). Following these two conventions, non-extensionists announced their own August convention in Buffalo, at which they intended to launch a new party.[34]

Barn-burner Democrats, 'Conscience' Whigs, and Liberty Party members met in convention on August 9, 1848 under the motto, "Free Soil, Free Speech, Free Labor, Free Men." They initiated the Free Soil Party. Although the new party supported only non-extension, its platform sought to please even the more radical Liberty Party men by requiring the federal government to abolish slavery wherever it had the power to do so. Party leaders declared, "No more slave states, no more slavery territory and no more compromises with slavery anywhere."[35]

The Liberty Party people, however—especially Gerrit Smith— were not happy with the Free Soil effort. For one thing, Free-Soilers did not favor the total abolition of slavery; even worse, their appeal was, in itself, racist. They sought no endorsements from blacks at the 1848 convention. Even though Frederick Douglass was in attendance, he was allowed to say only a few words because, according to one delegate, "they didn't want a nigger to talk to them."

Douglass blandly called the convention a "step in the right direction." He also noted that the real effort of the Free Soil party was to maintain the territories for white people, free of blacks—a position designed to attract northern votes. As Douglass put it, the party's efforts were aimed "not for the extension of liberty to the black man, but for the protection of liberty for the whites."[36]

The August Free Soil Party Convention displeased black leaders so much that they called their own convention in September in Cleveland, nominated Douglass for president, and rejected a resolution to support Free Soil candidates. Douglass complained that the Free Soil movement has "swallowed up the Liberty Party press and weakened its once powerful testimony against slavery."[37]

Although Free Soil Party presidential candidate and former President Martin VanBuren did not receive any electoral votes in 1848, the effort did set the stage for a future sectional party. And it demonstrated the weakening of voters' loyalties to both the Democratic and Whig parties.[38]

The advent of the Free Soil Party framed the slavery question in clear outlines. Voters could indicate whether they were for or against maintaining slavery—or, as Smith put it, extending freedom. The new party did not endorse the old Liberty Party's emphasis on the equality of all persons, and did not write a platform plank for equal rights. Free-Soilism opposed only the extension of slavery into new territory, thereby diluting the abolitionists' message to a lower standard and causing it to appeal to people who were less committed to abolition. Both the emancipation of all slaves and the equal rights issue were played down in order to attract votes from a wider racist constituency.

Obviously, the Free Soil Party was not an abolition party. It sought only to quarantine slavery where it already existed; its leaders demonstrated no moral aversion to it. Free Soilers generally saw abolition as a threat to white freedom, and they opposed the enfranchisement of black males. Their idea was that northerners should not tamper with southern institutions.[39]

The Free Soil Party never did have a large national impact by itself, so it appeared that antislavery political efforts were falling apart in the early 1850s. In truth, Democrats and Whigs were defecting to Free Soil orientations, thereby intensifying sectional divisions and encouraging abolitionists to persist ever more actively. The elections to the U.S. Senate of outspoken antislavery men like Benjamin Wade of Ohio and Charles Sumner of Massachusetts, and of Gerrit Smith to the House of Representatives, were symptomatic of the sectional split. Their voices clashed with the entrenched voices of Slave Power, making relevant issues vivid to the public ear.

One of the next signs that sectional division would lead to a coalition antislavery party came in Massachusetts following the election of 1848. Free-Soilers and Barn-burner Democrats forged a union based on the non-extension of slavery as a technique for challenging the dominant Whig Party in that state. This coalition resulted in Sumner's election to the U.S. Senate, and it became a model for third-party efforts that would follow. By 1852, the new organization had begun to call itself the Free Democratic Party. It held its nominating convention in Pittsburgh in mid-August. Non-extensionist New Hampshire Senator John P. Hale won the nomination for president, with former Whig George Julian from Indiana as vice president.

Gerrit Smith attended the convention and received a few votes as presidential nominee. Smith's major contribution to the convention came through his writings for the resolutions committee. Its resolutions included support for the Wilmot Proviso, denunciation of the Fugitive Slave Law with a call for its repeal, and the assertion that slavery was a sin. But the party rejected a resolution calling for political equality for free blacks; this led Smith to regard the party as just another racist party. In response, he called a convention of the Liberty Party in Syracuse that nominated William Goodell for president.[40]

Although the Free Democratic Party results in the 1852 election were disappointing, its efforts did keep sectional issues before the public eye. And the party served as a catalyst for the merging of 'Conscience' Whigs, Barn-burner Democrats, Free Democrats, Free-Soilers, Liberty Party, and Liberty League or Radical Abolition Party members into the Republican Party in 1854.

Several forces led these diverse factions to coalesce. After the 1852 election, the Whig Party appeared to be dead—especially after the deaths of Daniel Webster and Henry Clay, two important leaders. The Democratic Party had turned its gaze southward due to its support of slavery. Harriet Beecher Stowe's "Uncle Tom's Cabin," published in 1852, was selling well and was rallying many northern families to the cause of emancipation. And the 1850 Fugitive Slave Law had acted as a recruiting tool for northern antislavery votes.

Even a still-apolitical Gerrit Smith had, in 1852, won a seat in the U.S. House of Representatives—although he had not sought public office. Whereas abolitionists hailed Smith's election as a significant northern victory for the antislavery movement, Smith probably won the seat largely based on his support for a tariff reciprocity proposal with Canada that attracted business-oriented voters in his Upstate New York district.

By 1854, the old extension-of-slavery issue rang loudly in the debate over a bill in Congress supported by Democrats. Introduced by Democrat Stephen A. Douglas, the Kansas-Nebraska Bill was designed to nullify the previous non-extension of slavery agreement in the Missouri Compromise of 1820 by allowing state residents to decide through voting whether slavery should be approved locally.

As the debate proceeded in 1854, it became clear how powerful the pro-slavery forces were. Gerrit Smith, especially, was woefully out of place in Congress; he saw the Kansas-Nebraska Bill as an expression of moral indifference regarding racism, and although his public speech on the bill was one of his more brilliant and logical oratorical performances, it was inconsequential to the bill's passage into law. He even coauthored, with other antislavery-minded representatives and senators, a pamphlet to be printed in newspapers titled, "Appeal of the Independent Democrats in Congress to the People of the United States—Shall Slavery be Permitted in Nebraska?" In it, the writers questioned if Nebraska should be "convert[ed] into a dreary region of despotism, inhabited by masters and slaves."[41]

Although most of the antislavery senators and representatives stayed in Washington, D.C. to continue the battle, Gerrit Smith resigned his seat after one year to return to Peterboro, where he thought he could have more influence in establishing a model antislavery community for national emulation.

Whereas Smith's brand of antislavery politics did succeed in electing some local officials in central New York, it did not achieve success at the state or national level. Yet it did influence the coalition building process that would capture the White House in 1860.

Political events in the 1850s had given credence to the notion that antislavery forces were losing strength; but in fact, their real effect was the opposite. For instance, The Fugitive Slave Act of 1850 reinforced slave owners' ability to recapture runaway slaves, but it so infuriated northerners that it acted as an antislavery recruiting tool. The burning of Lawrence, KS by pro-slavery interests, and the caning of abolitionist senator Charles Sumner on the Senate floor by pro-slavery Congressman Preston Brooks—both on May 21, 1856—alerted antislavery people to the need for action. The Supreme Court decision in the 1857 Dred Scott case endorsed federal government support for slavery, but it angered those who viewed human rights as inherent in all persons. The 1854 Kansas-Nebraska Act nullified previous antislavery decisions, and led to the formation of new political coalitions. Sumner characterized it as

> "the best bill on which Congress ever acted, for it annuls all past compromises with slavery and makes any future compromise impossible. Thus it puts Freedom and Slavery face to face and bids them grapple. Who can doubt the result?"[42]

The North answered this sequence of events with a coalition of antislavery factions known as the Republican Party that nominated its first presidential candidate in 1856. John C. Frémont lost the election to Democrat Party candidate James Buchanan, but the stage was set for a contest in 1860 that would pit pro-slavery and antislavery forces against one another. This new Republican Party had the advantage of being free of identity with old parties, thus clearing itself of any responsibility for past defeats or mistakes.[43]

The Republican Party in 1860 held a position on antislavery issues that was very weak and did not please serious abolitionists. It favored the containment of slavery to areas where it already existed, but it did not support its abolition. Wendell Phillips called Lincoln "a half-converted, honest Western Whig, trying to be an abolition-ist." Indeed, Lincoln's positions regarding slavery seemed equivocal and only lukewarm. He was against the capture of runaway slaves, but would nevertheless enforce the 1850 law. He opposed slavery, but thought it to be legitimate if local residents approved of it. He opposed racial discrimination, but believed that blacks should re-main subordinate to whites.

Lincoln was not opposed to raising the social status of blacks; he just did not want to change positions with them. His main mo-tive was political expediency. As a 'compromise' candidate, he satis-fied moderates because he had not opposed slavery. And he satisfied radicals (if only mildly) because at least he opposed the extension of slavery. In 1860, his position balanced the political loyalties of vari-ous factions in the nation by placing a higher priority on preserving the Union than on the abolition of slavery. This was a masterful political ploy, because Lincoln did not alienate anyone completely. Even the abolitionists 'held their noses' and voted for him.[44]

Despite these discrepancies, most abolitionists agreed with Sumner that Lincoln "was the recognized political leader of those who sought the destruction of slavery...." In spite of some of Lin-coln's personal views, the Republican Party took an egalitarian stance in 1860 that was attractive to abolitionists, who had ma-tured through their radical phase to a more inclusive stance. Being less radical in their demands for immediate abolition, they became more appealing to northerners. As the northern economy's manu-facturing base became increasingly diversified, it required southern markets for its goods. But the stagnating effects of southern slavery were detrimental to northern profits, so more northerners were becoming sympathetic to the cause of abolition.[45]

Even the apolitical Garrison saw credibility in the Republican Party approach. He viewed their candidates as politicians who had endorsed moral principles rather than moral advocates who had stooped to adopt political tactics. Besides, he was tired—as were many other abolitionists after 30 years of work. Abolitionist Parker Pillsbury would later refer to the antislavery movement as the "Thirty years war before one shot was fired." They were ready to vote for Lincoln as the best candidate under circumstances that would not allow a radical abolitionist to be elected.

They knew that success in achieving the non-extension of slavery was not akin to achieving the abolition of slavery, but it was an acceptable half step. As Garrison had asked, would stopping the spread of a cancer cure it?[46]

The election of 1860 made it clear that the greatest fear of the abolitionists was about to come true: war seemed inevitable. Lincoln was elected on purely regional grounds, and the South was about to respond with secession and bullets. This was, however, no surprise to those who had spent decades trying to achieve change through either moral suasion or political action. Many of the abolitionists, in fact, had seen the eventual necessity of violence early in their crusade, but they held onto optimism and hoped that they were wrong.

They were not wrong.

~ 7 ~

Violence

Moral considerations have long since been exhausted upon slaveholders. It is vain to reason with them. One might as well hunt bears with ethics.... Slavery is a system of brute force.... It must be met with its own weapons.

- Frederick Douglass, 1859

I have come to despair of the peaceful termination of slavery. It must go out in blood. The time for abolishing it at the ballot-box has gone by—never to return.

- Gerrit Smith, 1856

By the late 1850s the fires of moral suasion and abolition politics had nearly burned out, and many abolitionists were willing to consider violence as a solution to the continued existence of slavery. But during the previous two decades, there were few who had done so. John Brown was an obvious exception.

The gathering of forces that led toward the acceptance of violence began to gain credence around the critical year of 1837. By that time, mob violence against abolitionists had convinced some of them that non-resistance was an ineffective response to intense racial prejudice in the North. Southern slaveholders' capital investment in slaves—second only to the amount invested in land—caused them to dig in their heels against northern opposition to slavery.[1]

The Panic of 1837 stifled economic growth, causing many in the general public to be so concerned about personal situations that it became difficult to recruit them to the cause of abolition. The effect of the economic downturn on budding abolitionists, however, was to highlight the predicament of the poor—especially blacks—and to cause them to regard affluence as unjust. Gerrit Smith became disillusioned by his trust in social stability. He began to imagine himself as a "colored person" and set off to foster the development of a new and more just social world. He began to see the use of violence by blacks as a legitimate tactic against the entrenched power of white supremacy, and by abolitionists as a righteous means of pursuing their grievance against slavery.

The murder of antislavery journalist Elijah Lovejoy by proslavery opponents in Alton, Illinois in November of 1837 was a major stimulant to the adoption of violence as a necessary antislavery tactic. In response to that event, John Brown dedicated his life to the destruction of slavery, and Wendell Phillips became actively involved in antislavery work in the Boston area. Shortly before his death, Lovejoy had written about his fear of violence against him. But he maintained that "...if I am to die, it cannot be in a better cause."[2]

In spite of their generally non-violent stance, most abolitionists understood that eventually the use of violence would be necessary. Gerrit Smith joined the newly formed American Peace Society in 1838, contributed $500 to its support, and became one of its vice-presidents in 1839. Even so, he remarked in a letter to John Quincy Adams in July of 1839 that, although he intended to pursue peaceful means toward abolition, "my prevailing apprehension is, that violence will accomplish the overthrow." For the next two decades, Smith would deal with inner turmoil over his desire for a peaceful end to slavery and his realization that he was becoming a supporter of the use of violence.[3]

Hoping for a peaceful solution, Smith and many other abolitionists initially supported moral suasion, politics, and legal action to gain ground against slavery. They favored legislation to abolish slavery where possible. They sought compromise between northern and southern sections of the country, and favored court cases and special "provisos" that might limit the spread of slavery. Even the effort to maintain political balance in Congress between "slave" and "free" states worked for a while. But the signs were clear that sectional division emphasizing deep cultural disagreements was becoming more and more important as a harbinger of future events.

One of those signs was the expanding development and increasing use of the underground railroad. Slaves had always tried to escape whether they lived in the North or the South, but two major developments in the early 1800s improved their prospects for success. First was the establishment of free states in the North. By 1830 most northern states had abolished slavery, so those slaves wishing to escape had a viable destination. Second, an elaborate "network to freedom" of sympathetic people and "stations," or safe houses, was becoming more available and complex, thus allowing escapees more secure and safe routes north.

The underground railroad recognized and emphasized glaring cultural differences between the North and the South and attracted much public attention to the injustice of racial discrimination. The fact that it even existed made a loud moral statement about a corrupt nation, and the irony that it highlighted was overwhelming. As one author put it, the process accomplished "the surreptitious transfer of human chattels from slavery in a free country to freedom in a monarchy."

Wendell Phillips said of John Brown's efforts to move escapees north, "he... passed his human protégés from the vulture of the United States to the safe shelter of the English lion...."[4]

The entire exercise of the underground railroad was a form of violence against slavery. Slaves stole property—themselves, and often owners' horses, clothing, or money—and ran toward free territory, helped by people who knowingly broke state and federal laws in the process. If threatened with capture, runaways fought back, claiming death to be more acceptable than a return to slavery. In fact, suicide was frequent among slaves—both in bondage and on the escape road. Bondage offered such a horrible life that the number of slaves who killed themselves and/or their children probably equaled the number who escaped.[5]

The national culture discriminated so intensely against blacks that underground railroad conductor Harriet Tubman commented,

"I wouldn't trust Uncle Sam with my people no longer, [so] I brought 'em clear off to Canada."

Even in the South, some people wondered about the morality of slavery. South Carolina diarist Mary Chestnut mused,

"I wonder if it be a sin to think slavery a curse to any land.... God forgive us, but ours is a monstrous system + wrong...."[6]

Knowledge that they had slim chances for freedom stimulated resistance among slaves, and instances of individual and collective rebellion increased. As slaveholders became paranoid regarding the possibility of violence coming from their own "happy and well-treated darkies," they began to perceive the North as typified by the militant John Brown and reacted with threats to anyone who supported abolition. The Georgia State Legislature offered $4,000 for the arrest of William Lloyd Garrison; New York City abolitionist Arthur Tappan had a price on his head of $12,000 in Macon, GA and $20,000 in New Orleans. A vigilance committee in South Carolina offered $1,500 for the arrest of anyone distributing Garrison's antislavery newspaper <u>The Liberator</u>. Antislavery literature was confiscated and burned from a Charleston, South Carolina post office; in Georgia and South Carolina, some whites were murdered for the "crime" of mixing with blacks in public.[7]

As northern agitation for abolition increased, the South desperately grasped for any indication that its lifestyle would be supported. In a mid-1840s effort to acquire new territory for the expansion of slavery, proslavery President James K. Polk succeeded in getting Congress to declare war with Mexico in order to forcefully acquire the territories of New Mexico, Utah, and California. The plan worked, and it reopened the slavery debate that had been temporarily quelled by the Missouri Compromise of 1820. Gerrit Smith saw the irony in the Missouri Compromise quite clearly: he called it a "fatal mistake" because it legitimated slavery where it existed.

> "It... dignified, and emboldened slavery. From that day to this slavery has felt itself to be a power in the land—an admitted and respectable power. Its claims to at least an equal standing and an equal share with liberty are put forth everywhere, and acknowledged everywhere...."

The results of this, Smith said, were that

> "From the sad hour, when Slavery triumphed over Freedom in the Missouri Compromise, down to the present no sadder hour, she has never ceased to be a ruined nation."

Feeling some vindication, backers of the Slave Power of the South marshaled their forces to fight the national legislative battle that would become known as the Compromise of 1850.[8]

When it became clear in 1850 that California would be admitted to the growing nation as a free state, the South demanded balance by pushing for a strengthened fugitive slave law as a means of dealing more successfully with increasing numbers of runaway slaves.

In accordance with the original Fugitive Slave Act of 1793, runaway slaves could be legally captured in free states prior to 1850, but there were no penalties to northerners for harboring them. What the South wanted was a validation of the institution of slavery where it existed as a repudiation of the moral claims of the North-based abolition movement. The Compromise of 1850 bill was a complicated document, only part of which dealt with fugitive slaves. The Congressional debate over the bill lasted for ten months, still with no agreement on the entire package of provisions.

The portion of the bill that became labeled The Fugitive Slave Act of 1850 passed in the Senate on August 26 by a vote of 27 to 12, and in the House of Representatives on September 12 by a vote of 109 to 76. It was signed into law by President Millard Fillmore on September 18, 1850.[9]

On the dates of August 21 and 22, while the bill was still being debated, abolitionists held a protest convention in the central New York village of Cazenovia. The convention was organized by Frederick Douglass and Gerrit Smith and was attended by so many people—including approximately 40 former slaves—that it had to be moved from the local Free Church to a nearby apple orchard. Its purpose was to highlight the infuriation felt by many northerners over the notion that alien slave owners would be allowed to pursue their human property on northern soil, and that northerners themselves would be expected to aid them.[10]

The provisions of the law threatened both blacks and whites. Fugitive slaves were obviously in danger, but even free blacks were threatened with capture and sale into slavery by greedy and unscru-

The Cazenovia Convention picture includes Frederick Douglass (to left of table with elbow on table); Theodosia Gilbert (lady keeping notes at center of table; also identified as Abby Kelley Foster, but Foster may have been in Ohio at the time); Joseph Hathaway (at right end of table taking notes); Mary Edmonson (black woman in shawl behind Gilbert); Gerrit Smith (standing at center, arm out); Emily Edmonson (black woman in shawl to right of Gerrit Smith); George W. Clark (standing just over the right side of Emily Edmonson's shoulder); Samuel J. May (just behind Joseph Hathaway); Charles B. Ray (to the right of May); and James Caleb Jackson (to the right of Ray). Identifications by Hugh Humpreys.

Photo used with the permission of the Madison County Historical Society pulous slave catchers. As a federal law, it gave marshals authority to deputize any citizen to help catch fugitives. Citizens who refused to help or aided a fugitive in any way were subject to fines of $1,000 (the equivlent of about $70,000 today) and imprisonment for up to six months. Proof of ownership of a slave required only an affidavit from the claimant, and the slave had no right to testify and no right to a jury trial. If a captured fugitive was set free, the marshal would be paid $5. If the slave was sent back into slavery, $10 was the marshal's payment.[11]

Northerners viewed the law as a threat to everyone's freedom that would bring further erosion of liberties if it was not challenged. Abolitionists denounced the law and vowed to see that it could not be enforced. The law forced people to face the dilemma of honoring either national law or natural law, and many felt that they could not obey the new law without losing their self-respect. Joshua Giddings, a 'Conscience' Whig senator from Ohio, proclaimed, "Let the President... use the bayonet, the sword and the cannon.... Let him drench our land of freedom in blood; but he will never make us obey that law." Black underground railroad station master Robert Purvis threatened to kill any person who attempted to execute the law on him.[12]

The signing of the Fugitive Slave Law served to emphasize and strengthen sectional attitudes. 'Cotton' Whig Robert Winthrop commented,

> "Never in the history of our country... has there been a party which under the pretext of philanthropy, has so reveled and luxuriated in malice, hatred and uncharitableness, in vituperation, calumny and slander as this reviled Free Soil sect."

'Conscience' Whig Charles Francis Adams referred to the signing of the law in these terms: "The consummation of the inequities of the most disgraceful session of Congress is now reached."[13]

In the early 1850s, abolitionists responded by conducting a series of dramatic rescues of captured fugitive slaves. One such event—the "Jerry Rescue"—took place in Syracuse, New York on October 1, 1851.

In a violent act of defiance of federal law, a number of local abolitionists led by Gerrit Smith forcibly entered the building where a captured fugitive slave named Jerry was being held by police. Jerry was successfully rescued and escorted to freedom in Canada. In order to humiliate public authorities, some Syracuse women connected with the abolition movement sent thirty pieces of silver to the government's prosecuting attorney, thereby placing him in the Judas-like role of traitor to a higher cause. The rescuers thus succeeded in publicizing the inhumanity of slavery.[14]

The irony of the Fugitive Slave Act of 1850 is that in the long run, it achieved very little success in returning runaway slaves to their previous owners. But it achieved a great deal of success in making abolitionism respectable in the North and in recruiting many previously complacent northerners into the abolition movement. Wendell Phillips saw the law as "a slaveholders' triumph disguised as a compromise," but he recognized the fact that it performed well in stimulating northern interest in abolition.[15]

Frederick Douglass spoke against the law at a protest meeting in Boston's Faneuil Hall, highlighting the law's influence in fostering post-revolutionary thinking. By encouraging a confrontation between authority and ethics, the law encouraged a legitimate role for violence in opposition to it.[16]

The Jerry Rescue violence in Syracuse had negated Daniel Webster's promise made in that city on May 26, 1851 to ensure the enforcement of the Fugitive Slave Act. He had assailed abolitionists for their "higher law" advocacy, and found that much of the public was soundly behind them. Following the Jerry Rescue, the new law met with no attempts to enforce it in central and western New York. Fugitive slaves were relatively safe there, and antislavery politics grew in popularity and attracted local leaders.[17]

The general public attitude was reflected in a resolution made by Syracusans at an anti-fugitive slave law conference: "it is our duty to peril life, liberty, and property, in behalf of the fugitive slave, to as great an extent, as we could peril them in behalf of ourselves." Such opinion was championed and led by central New York abolitionist leaders like Jermain Wesley Loguen in Syracuse, Gerrit Smith in Peterboro (east of Syracuse), and Frederick Douglass in Rochester (west of Syracuse).[18]

The black population of Syracuse had already set the base for such public opinion in a September 23, 1850 convention in the African Congregation Church at which they declared,

> "We the colored citizens of Syracuse will join hand in hand, and will take the scalp of any government hound that dares follow on our track as we are resolved to be free...."

They favored violence instead of flight:

> "We repudiate the idea of flight for these reasons: first that we have committed no crime against the law of the land, second resistance to Tyrants is obedience to God, and third that liberty which is not worth defending here is not worth enjoying anywhere."[19]

What blacks were perceiving clearly was the intensity of racial prejudice in the North. Wendell Phillips noted that "Northern opinion [i.e., racism] is the opiate of Southern conscience." Even Abraham Lincoln stated his personal brand of racism clearly in an 1858 debate with Stephen Douglas:

> "I am not, nor ever have been, in favor of bringing about in any way the social and political equality of the white

and black races.... And inasmuch as... they do remain together there must be the position of superior and inferior, and I as much as any other man am in favor of having the superior position assigned to the white race."[20]

Probably almost no northerner was free of racial prejudice—even the abolitionists. They realized that they faced enormous dissonance in reconciling their desire for a peaceful solution with their growing approval of violence. Gerrit Smith, for instance, financially supported vigilance committees, radical antislavery newspapers, and John Brown—yet tried to pacify the situation by supporting compensated emancipation—all at the same time in the mid-1850s. He even cynically suggested that it was whites that needed to be removed from the nation to a new colony as "treatment" of their intense prejudice.[21]

The non-violent stance of most abolitionists of the 1830s had changed by the 1850s. Events like the death of Lovejoy, the caning of Sumner, the burning of Pennsylvania Hall and the passage of the Fugitive Slave Act had focused the abolitionists' gaze on the egalitarian goals of the American Revolution, turning their opposition to slavery into a patriotic act. Their new "spirit of '76" fueled their old dreams of perfection with renewed optimism that interpreted violence as an acceptable means of operation. Thus they solved the dissonance problem of the sin of violence vs. morality by making "righteous violence" a moral act.

What resulted was essentially an extensive program of "civil disobedience" throughout the North. Vigilance Committees to protect fugitive slaves from federal law were established in many communities; legal counsel was offered to fugitives; slave catchers and owners were harassed; and even slave rescues by force multiplied. Rescues, in fact, became a dramatic expression of the intensity of antislavery emotion.[22]

After the Jerry Rescue, Gerrit Smith opted for the conviction of United States Deputy Marshal Henry W. Allen for kidnapping, and claimed that the 1850 law was unconstitutional because it offended human morality based in natural law that prohibited the ownership of people as property. Similar forcible rescues of former slaves Joshua Glover in Wisconsin and John Price in Ohio also served to attract public attention and empathy.[23]

Other acts of civil disobedience encouraged confrontation and defiance. On July 4, 1854 in Framingham, Massachusetts, William Lloyd Garrison publicly burned a copy of the Fugitive Slave Act of 1850, a copy of the court order for the return to slavery of escaped slave Anthony Burns, and a copy of the United States Constitution. Later, a convention of abolitionists in Worcester, Mass. called for national disunion as a technique of thwarting the proslavery stance of the federal government. All such acts were forecasting more intense violence to come.[24]

The 1850 law had dashed hopes for a peaceful approach to ending slavery that had been kindled by the Wilmot Proviso and the Free Soil Party, thus encouraging antislavery people to adopt different means of pursuing their goal. Abolitionist Henry Highland Garnet in Troy, New York started carrying a pistol for self-defense. Boston lawyer and abolitionist Lysander Spooner began advocating a plan of inciting insurrection among slaves in the South, and even Wendell Phillips agreed. Phillips also knew that some of his Boston friends were members of the "Secret Six" along with Gerrit Smith—a group of abolitionists who were supporting John Brown. Phillips showed no opposition.[25]

Supporting or encouraging violence could be very expensive for white abolitionists. Black abolitionists were almost expected to advocate violence because they felt and understood more clearly the violence that had kept them or "their people" in slavery. But very few white abolitionists could develop enough empathy with slaves to feel "black" themselves. Traces of racist tendencies and connections with racist culture prevented them from identifying closely with black people. Two who did cross this racial divide were John Brown and Gerrit Smith.

Both men were called "crazy" or "mad". Their perspectives on humanity led them to break down the barriers that maintained separation between races. Their advocacy of the use of violence to pursue abolition eventually cost Smith a temporary loss of mental health, and Brown his life.

The focal point of early violence in support of abolition in the 1850s was Kansas Territory. In 1854 the Kansas-Nebraska Bill was debated at length in Congress. If passed, it would allow the residents there to vote on the issue of being admitted to the nation as a free or a slave state. Then-Congressman Gerrit Smith argued against it because of his concern that slavery might be extended into new territory. Abolitionists generally saw it as giving the people the right to choose the wrong idea, and they were dismayed that the bill carried the false idea that freedom and slavery were equal social systems.

When the bill became law, the idea of voting for either a free or slave labor economic system turned into a fight over the morality of liberty vs. slavery. Kansas became a testing ground for sectional cultural differences and a physical battleground for local civil war that predicted the conflagration that was soon to come. Smith believed that the Kansas-Nebraska Act would actually hasten the death of slavery because of growing public opposition to the spread of slavery. He wrote,

> "The tide of war once set in motion there [will] never subside, until it shall have overwhelmed and swept away the whole of American slavery."[26]

This renewal of action in Kansas brought back to activism some abolitionists who had been sitting it out for a while. Angelina

Grimké Weld welcomed violence in Kansas as predicting the end of slavery. She had previously warned, "It is manifest to every reflecting mind that slavery must be abolished.... Now, there are only two ways in which it can be effected, by moral power or physical force, and it is up to you [slave owners] to choose which of these you prefer."

Lydia Maria Child worked to help free soil families in Kansas. Thomas Wentworth Higginson traveled to Kansas and recommended military action to support Free-Soilers.

Minister Henry Ward Beecher also advocated military activity instead of moralizing, saying, "you might just as well read the Bible to buffaloes."

Gerrit Smith sponsored the donation of money and arms to John Brown for his "Kansas work" and provided over $16,000 ($1.2 million today) to send free soil families from New England to live in Kansas.[27]

John Brown's radical thought and his orientation toward action drew him to Kansas. He claimed that it was "nothing to die in a good cause, but an eternal disgrace to sit still in the presence of the barbarities of American slavery." He believed that he held "a commission direct from God Almighty to act against slavery," and he wrote that "an old man should have more care to end life well than to live long."[28]

Brown's self-certainty fueled a charisma that was a magnet to frustrated immediatists who had spent decades talking and voting. He was skilled at manipulating others to support his prophetic vision of ending slavery quickly—an attractive thought for those who agreed that they should fight for the cause of the weaker person. Brown's arrogance has often been misinterpreted as sociopathic. Actually, his actions made practical sense, and they exposed the fears of his observers that they might, if Brown's plan worked, lose their own privileged status.[29]

John Brown, as depicted in the Joe Flores illustration commissioned by the National Abolition Hall of Fame & Museum.

The clashes in Kansas between free soil and proslavery interests were often brutal. Free soil settlers were being killed. Their efforts to establish a liberty-based state government were intentionally subverted by proslavery President Franklin Pierce and by incursions of proslavery "voters" from the neighboring slave state of Missouri. Because John Brown was supportive of Free-Soilers, his life and those of his family members were threatened by former slave catcher Henry "Dutch" Sherman and James Doyle and his sons, William and Drury. Aware that he and his family were in imminent danger of being killed, Brown opted for a preemptive strike and killed his enemies first. As such, Brown's act at Pottawatomie was—as well stated by biographer Louis DeCaro, Jr.—"not an unprovoked act of unbridled anti-slavery rage or terrorism as it is often portrayed." Should we, he asks, call Brown a terrorist "while overlooking the fundamental terrorism of a nation that sustained and protected slavery[?]"[30]

Because the proslavery regime in Kansas that had been installed through corruption would not enforce protective law for Free-Soilers, Brown declared that something must be done to show the strength of the free state opposition and quell the proslavery terrorists and actions. His response was based in experience and evidence, not in illogical fanaticism.[31]

In retrospect, the entire scene that played out in Kansas territory in the 1850s was an exercise in irony. Although it was extremely violent—as Brown biographer David Reynolds points out—it was not the right location for violence to be able to solve the debate over slavery. The eastern area of the country was where intense prejudice and cultural clashes sought reconciliation. The western frontier of Kansas was destined to be free territory for a number of social and geographical reasons. The abolitionists worried deeply and expended resources lavishly on the Kansas area in their attempts to keep it free of slavery. John Brown, for instance, risked his life and the lives of some of his sons there for years. Gerrit Smith spent $16,000 to help free soil families migrate from New England to the Kansas Territory. Their fear that popular sovereignty would result in more slave states was ill-founded.[32]

Kansas was admitted to the Union as a free state in 1861 for reasons that probably had little do with the efforts of abolitionists. The idea of popular sovereignty as applied to the western territories was actually an antislavery philosophy. The new settlers there came mostly from the northern states of Illinois, Indiana, and Ohio. Only 4% were former New Englanders, so Smith's huge financial effort was largely wasted.[33]

The new settlers brought with them a love for liberty and for self-determination. Available land as a source of security and potential wealth attracted independent minds. Economically marginal people could migrate to Kansas Territory with an axe and a rifle, whereas the slave owner was encumbered by his own institution. It was very difficult to transplant slavery because the entire conservative institution would need to move intact, and without proper soil conditions or supportive social structure, its success was far from guaranteed. Because slavery might not be established in Kansas, there was no security for slave owners' property, so most of them chose not to take the risk. By 1860, most of the settlers who had arrived were interested in establishing a culture based on free labor and independence that could leave for their children a legacy of freedom and equal opportunity. Such ideas conquered both the frontier wilderness and slavery.[34]

Perhaps the big lesson to come from the 1850s in Kansas Territory was that the Slave Power had become too weak to secure what it wanted on a national scale. Ideas related to free labor—liberty, freedom, and the inherent human right to self-determination—were marching on from the Revolutionary era in the enlightened minds of the masses in the mid-19th century. As Gerrit Smith put it,

> "What a wonder, what a shame, what a crime, that, in the midst of the light and progress of the middle of the nineteenth century, such an abomination and outrage as slavery, should be acknowledged to be a legal institution."[35]

The tragedy of "bleeding Kansas" lay not in the fact that violence occurred there, but in the failure of the country as a whole to be able to overcome its sectional prejudices by witnessing the lessons that Kansas illustrated. It was now clear that slavery could not prevail over freedom. But prejudice dies hard. Attitudes—as the moral suasionists could testify—do not change in response to logic. Unfortunately, violence still had a role to play, and its instrument was John Brown.

Brown's purpose in capturing the Federal arsenal at Harpers Ferry, VA is probably best stated by one of his Kansas compatriots. James Redpath spent time with Brown in Kansas, fighting against proslavery interests. He wrote about events surrounding Brown—including Harpers Ferry—as early as 1860, before Brown's actions had become widely misinterpreted by a vengeful society. Redpath commented that Brown's raiders

> "sought no offensive warfare against the South, but only to restore to the African race its inherent rights, by enabling it to demand them of its oppressors, with the power to enforce and maintain the claim. Not revolution, but justice; not aggression, but defense; not negro supremacy, but citizenship; not war <u>against</u> society, but <u>for</u> freedom...."[36]

John Kagi, a member of Brown's Harpers Ferry party, spoke of Brown's plan as a show of northern support designed to inspire slaves to join a slowly expanding opposition throughout the Virginia mountains. Operating by means of guerrilla tactics, its purpose would be to inject paranoia into the minds of slave owners, thereby destabilizing the institution of slavery. Over time, as more and more former slaves, free blacks, and sympathetic whites joined in supporting the goal of freedom for slaves, a network of antislavery centers could be established in the mountains to facilitate the movement of people toward the North.[37]

According to Redpath, Brown had known "for many years" that his initial point of attack against slavery would be at Harpers Ferry. Brown never told this fact to many people because he feared that they were actually not radical enough to accept its implications of treason against the United States, or were not sufficiently accepting of the use of violence that might result in death. Gerrit Smith, in fact, denied until his death in 1874 that he knew of the specific point of attack before it occurred. Kagi asserted that

> "no politician, in the Republican party or any other party, knew of their plans, and but few of the abolitionists. It was no use talking of Anti-slavery <u>action</u> to Non-resistant Agitators."[38]

In accordance with these first-hand statements, it appears that Brown's purpose for the raid was <u>not</u> to incite insurrection or to free slaves directly, but to put slaves in a position of being more likely to secure their own freedom. He wished to develop a climate of fear among slave owners and optimism among slaves regarding the potential success of escape. Brown hoped that as some slaves escaped the South, they would incite others to do so, resorting to violence only in defense of their liberty. His goal in the long run was "to drain slavery of its economic vitality" so that it would die without violence.[39]

Brown did realize before his death by hanging, however, that widespread and brutal violence would be necessary before slavery could end. But his Harpers Ferry raid was so successful in producing paranoia throughout the South that even the reassurance of newly elected President Abraham Lincoln that he had no intention of interfering with slavery in states where it already existed could not quell the southern states' intent to secede from the Union.[40]

The role most of the abolitionists played in the support of John Brown was pathetic. Even though most of them realized by the late 1850s that violence would be necessary to end slavery, and although they knew Brown to be the person to instigate it, they could not bring themselves to openly support him. The "Secret Six" who did support Brown felt that they must be clandestine about it. Brown did what the abolitionists had been trying to do for thirty years: he struck a blow at an immoral society. But only after the fact did he receive accolades from abolitionists, and even then, people admired him more for his guts to do something than for his moral stand.[41]

As for Gerrit Smith, the violence at Harpers Ferry struck a serious blow to his regard for himself. He suddenly felt very guilty that he had abandoned his long commitment to peace and non-violence, and for a brief time, he lost his grip on reality. Because delusions and hallucinations plagued him, his family decided to admit him to the Utica Insane Asylum. Dr. John P. Gray used a pattern of treatment that included mind-altering drugs, diet change, and social change by keeping him removed from the environment that had contributed to the ailment. Seven weeks later, Gray accompanied Smith on his return to his Peterboro home and advised family and staff members in prudent techniques of care.[42]

Smith never again experienced the "mania" he exhibited in late 1859, but neither did he ever reconcile his approval of violence with personal concern for the peaceful resolution of issues. Smith's case illustrates vividly what many other abolitionists felt at least minimally; that is, because it was violence that succeeded in destabilizing slavery and assuring its eventual demise, the moral lesson intended was obscured.

As Frederick Douglass put it,

> "Liberty came to the freedmen of the United States, not in mercy, but in wrath, not by moral choice, but by military necessity...."

Because the racist attitudes of Americans had not changed when the Civil War ended, the work of abolition would continue.[43]

Although most abolitionists had supported the Civil War, many of them found it difficult to do so. Gerrit Smith serves as a model here. Having tried to solve the slavery problem by means of persuasion or politics, he came reluctantly to support violence. It offended his sense of moral purity and obstructed his personal effort to set an example for all people. Even though he knew of the success of the violent Haitian revolution against slavery in the 1790s, he felt that he had failed both himself and the social reform effort. Therefore, he felt guilty. Smith's support of violence was somewhat artificial, unlike that of Brown who had long stated his intent to use it. Although Brown had received support from Smith in both words and money for over a decade, Brown could sense Smith's timidity, and so he refused to reveal the full details of his plan to Smith for fear that he would withdraw.[44]

What had become clear by 1860 to those who had some feeling for the abolition movement was that sectionally based violence on a national scale was imminent. Some even welcomed it. Wendell Phillips analyzed the North and South positions and said,

> "After drifting, a dreary sight of thirty years, before the hurricane, our ship of State is going to pieces on the lee shore of slavery."

Phillips approved of the Civil War as a way to provoke disunion, and he believed that the superior industrial power of the North would overrun southern culture. He became upset—as did many of the abolitionists—with Lincoln's management of the war. He called the president a "first rate second rate man" for putting salvation of the Union with slavery above emancipation.

Smith was disgusted with Lincoln for trying to save the Union instead of abolishing slavery. "The South," he said, "would never have made the War had not Slavery first made her mad." He criticized Lincoln for overrating the importance of constitutional action in time of war, and for the conciliation of supposedly loyal slaveholders. In order to unite abolitionists against Lincoln's reluctance to fight the war to end slavery, the Emancipation League was formed in 1861. Lincoln did eventually hear the call for abolition— but slowly.[45]

By 1861, emancipation was gaining credence as a possible way to avoid a long and costly war. Soon after the 37th Congress opened its first session on December 2, 1861, Massachusetts representative Thomas Eliot proposed that the commander-in-chief use martial law to emancipate all slaves; Pennsylvania representative James Campbell proposed confiscation of slaves as property employed in war; Pennsylvania representative Thaddeus Stevens proposed that Lincoln declare as free all slaves who aided the North in the war. Such agitation certainly had some influence on the president.[46]

In March of 1862, Lincoln proposed to Congress an emancipation plan by which states would be compensated for "inconveniences" produced by the results of gradual emancipation. The bill was designed to persuade southern states to abolish slavery by choice. Lincoln's generals, prosecuting the war in the field, felt an immediate need for emancipation of the slaves. In August of 1861, General John C. Frémont declared martial law in his army command area in Missouri and abolished slavery there. General David Hunter proclaimed that all slaves in his area of command in South Carolina, Georgia, and Florida were free as of May 9, 1862. Lincoln voided both orders as he worked on issuing a more broadly-based proclamation.[47]

On July 17, 1862, Congress passed the Second Confiscation Act, declaring slaves inside of Union lines to be free. Congressional leaders urged President Lincoln to emancipate all slaves. Earlier, in April of 1862, Lincoln had signed an emancipation act for the District of Columbia. When his Emancipation Proclamation was announced on September 22, 1862, it met with mixed public reaction. To blacks, it was no surprise; they had known that the war was about emancipation before Lincoln did. Abolitionists viewed it as a weak attempt to appease political forces. Because it freed slaves only in those states at war with the Union, Gerrit Smith saw it as a half-hearted step in the right direction, and he hoped that soon Lincoln would "do his whole duty."

Lincoln saw the proclamation as a military necessity—a way to rob enemy forces of an important tool of their war effort. Once freed, the former slaves would no longer work for the South as war laborers, and they could disobey rules set for them and openly disrespect former owners. While abolitionists wanted to shake Lincoln's hand in thanks, they hesitated because they did not want him to think that the job was finished. In fact, the abolitionists knew that even the war itself could not finish the job of emancipation.[48]

A new wave of antislavery activity broke out after the Civil War had started. The new antislavery effort was less of a moral concern for the rights of blacks than a fight against rebels who had wronged the nation. By seceding, the southern states had offered the North a way to abolish slavery; now they had become a foreign country at war. The sentiment that grew after Fort Sumter was more anti-southern than antislavery.

This bothered the old-guard abolitionists—especially the outspoken Frederick Douglass. He considered the abolition movement a failure because it had not succeeded at instilling a sense of righteous justice in the minds of most northerners. They now pursued emancipation for military or political reasons, not moral ones. People were finally doing the right thing, but for the wrong reasons, so Frederick Douglass could foresee frightening long-term problems with racial discrimination.

~ 8 ~

The Aftermath

Neither the rebellion nor slavery is yet ended. The rebellion has been disarmed; but that is all. Slavery has been abolished in name; but that is all.... The work of liberation is not yet completed.

- Charles Sumner, 1865

The fruits of ten years of labor, suffering and loss are at stake.... The slave demon still rides the southern gale, and breathes out fire and wrath.

- Frederick Douglass, 1872

As the Civil War dragged on in 1862, factions of abolitionists began to unite behind William Lloyd Garrison's attempt to rally forces against President Lincoln's weak antislavery stance. Gerrit Smith told Garrison that their differing interpretations of the United States Constitution could be ignored in favor of supporting immediate executive emancipation of the slaves. To emphasize his sincerity, he sent a $50 donation to the Garrisonian American Anti-Slavery Society. Even Frederick Douglass put aside past antagonisms to recognize all antislavery people as "kinsmen."[1]

Frederick Douglass, in the portrait by Joe Flores commissioned by the National Abolition Hall of Fame & Museum.

All three of these abolitionist giants viewed Lincoln's Emancipation Proclamation as a promissory note that only future moral change in the general population could fulfill. Being a legal instrument only, it could not free the white population of their racial bias, so the work of achieving freedom for all had not been concluded. It had only just begun.

The monumental task for both politicians and abolitionists in the 1860s, as so aptly stated by James Brewer Stewart, was how "to transform a civil war between two antagonistic civilizations into a revolution in race relations." In 1861, the 37th Congress made some proposals to get started with the task: diplomatic recognition of the black republic of Haiti; ban slavery in all new territories; repeal the 1850 Fugitive Slave Law. Actually, all of these were timid recommendations. No one proposed that slavery should be abolished completely. The radical Republicans could not overpower moderates who feared emancipation, so racism prevailed in both the Congress and the general public. Even before the Emancipation Proclamation was issued, Gerrit Smith worried,

> "It is true that were the slaveholders to emancipate under the pressure of War... they would then be both morally and physically unconquerable; the nation would be divided; and for a time, great evil would ensue both to the North and South."[2]

The goal of most Republicans, including President Lincoln, was to preserve the Union. The Republican coalition that had elected Lincoln was diverse and weak, and not ready to alienate all of the slave states. They needed to maintain the loyalty of free-soil voters, as well as the loyalties of the "border states" that, while they legitimized slavery, tended toward supporting union. It was not until 1864 that the Republican Party platform declared, for the first time in national history, that slavery was incompatible with a government founded and built upon the principles of democracy and freedom.[3]

On February 8, 1864, abolitionist Senator Charles Sumner introduced a bill to repeal all fugitive slave laws. After discussion and amendment, it passed in both houses by late June. He was also successful in helping to enact laws that suppressed the domestic slave trade. He removed the ban on black passengers on Washington, D.C. railroads, and abolished the exclusion of black testimony in United States courts.[4]

Although these successes allowed for some optimism concerning changes in race relations, it was not to be extended much further. After the assassination of President Lincoln, liberal-minded Republican politicians and abolitionists found themselves trapped

Senator Charles Sumner, R-Mass, was an outspoken
critic of slavery and fugitive slave laws.
Photo courtesy of the author

---

by the limits of an age of white supremacy. Former Vice President
Andrew Johnson took the reins of a Reconstruction effort designed
to foster equal rights for all citizens—and halted it. Sumner said of
the new president,

> "You must not forget that the President is a bad man, the
> author of incalculable woe to his county, and especially
> to that part which, being most tried by war, most needed
> kindly care. Search history, and I am sure you will find
> no elected ruler who, during the same short time, has
> done so much mischief to his country. He stands alone in
> bad eminence."[5]

Johnson supported the conservative effort of the South to
maintain white supremacy in spite of emancipation. He approved

of "black codes" in southern states designed to maintain inferior status for blacks, and he promoted efforts of the Slave Power to assert control over decision-making at all levels. Regarding the ability of the South to advance in achieving equity among all elements of its population, Sumner commented,

> "A community just conquered, demoralized by a long war, prostrated by the loss of property and lives, sullen, disloyal, and filled with hatred and contempt for the new freedmen and their own loyal white neighbors, was a hotbed in which trouble of every kind found root easily and grew rapidly.... Only the slow passage of years, the death of those too old to learn, the birth of a new generation, the replacement of men born slaves by men born free, could make these communities peaceful and prosperous. Friction between the two races in their new relation was inevitable."

Sumner knew that he could not depend on the political establishment to aid in relieving the suffocating influence of racism. Other abolitionists also saw the danger. Frederick Douglass warned,

> "Slavery has existed in this country too long and has stamped its character too deeply and indelibly to be blotted out in a day or a year or even in a generation. The slave will yet remain in some sense a slave long after the chains are taken from his limbs; and the master will retain much of the pride, arrogance, imperiousness, and love of power, acquired by his former position of master."

Gerrit Smith also advised the public,

> "'Reconstruction' is ample proof that the War has left us with a disposition toward the negro no better than

it was before the War, but, if possible, worse. The nation... is perishing because she persists in not letting the negro into the human family.... The nation clings to the wickedness [of race prejudice] and still refuses to open to the negro any of the strong-barred and century-rusted gates, which shut him out from the enjoyment of political and social rights.... He suffers at every turn and corner of human relations.... From the enslaved race they have become the hated race."[6]

In January 1866, Senator Lyman Trumbull introduced a bill to prevent discrimination based on race or color. After debate, the bill passed both houses of Congress. On March 27, President Andrew Johnson vetoed it. Although the Congress did override Johnson's veto, his action symbolized a national attitude. In the November 1874 elections, Democrats (the pro-racist party of the time) took over the Congress and elected nineteen state governors. Gerrit Smith foresaw this possibility:

"My dread [is that] the Democrats will be able to obtain a majority [in the national legislature]. And then our anti-slavery work with all its cost of treasure and tears and blood, will be undone, and our freedmen be surrendered to their old oppressors."

He wrote to newspaper editor Horace Greeley about the Democratic Party,

"For the last half century, the Democratic Party has planted itself immovably against our colored bretheren.... Do not forget its never-flagging and ever-bitter opposition to the abolition of slavery, and how intensely hostile it was to the Freedmen's Bureau, and to all other measures for enlightening and protecting the poor

Freedmen.... Do not forget how inflexibly it contended
against granting the ballot and equal civil rights to the
black man, both of the North and South."

Smith actually held contempt for both major political parties
after the war. He claimed that

"The positively bad character of the Democratic Party
is far more efficient to gain influence and votes than the
negatively and uncertainly good character of the Republican Party. The Democratic Party, daring to be unjust,
attracts by its courage. The Republican Party, not daring
to be just, is despised for its cowardice."

He believed that the Republican Party had failed.

"By their desertion of [blacks, Republicans] have dis-
graced themselves, disqualified themselves to be teachers,
cheapened the black man's rights, and made that heart
more flinty than ever.... [Blacks] may... be driven by a
sense of their wrongs to fearful and widespread violence."[7]

As if nationwide racist attitudes were not enough to hinder
progress toward equality, other trends were also at play. After 1865,
antislavery organizations at all levels began to dissolve. When the
thirteenth amendment to the United States Constitution abolished
slavery, it appeared to some that the work of the abolition movement
was completed. Many antislavery newspapers stopped publishing.
Garrison even terminated The Liberator, which had for over three
decades been one of the most radical sources of antislavery ideas
available for public consumption.

Garrison also proposed to dissolve the American Anti-Slavery
Society at the time. What he seemed to be ignoring was that the

third article of the constitution of that organization called for the elimination of race prejudice as one of its goals.

Many abolitionists were upset with Garrison because he seemed intent on removing from the social scene their base of power for being heard and for lobbying legislatures. When Garrison did actually pull out, Wendell Phillips took over and became president of the American Anti-Slavery Society. He received support in that role from such powerful abolitionists as Gerrit Smith, Frederick Douglass, Lucretia Mott, and others. They saw Garrison as abandoning the freedman at a time when he needed support to continue the "second abolition" fight against racial discrimination.[8]

The American Anti-Slavery Society continued its work only until 1870, when Phillips disbanded it following the ratification of the fifteenth amendment that provided for black male suffrage. It is doubtful that Phillips and his organizational colleagues believed that the work of the movement to eliminate discrimination was complete, but they were tired. After four decades of fighting against an intensely racist society, they were burned out. And as Americans became concerned about new industrial trends, new markets, and embraced the optimism of a war free nation, the abolitionists retreated into the background.

Gerrit Smith noted that abolitionists still had little credibility with the public. Having studied human rights all their lives, they had much to say about continued racial discrimination, but no one would listen. The need for support for the equitable treatment of blacks after the war lacked the original zeal and commitment of the crusading abolitionists. The antislavery editors, speakers, and politicians gave ground to tenacious white supremacists, and "Reconstruction" faltered.

When the aging abolitionists wrote their autobiographies in the 1870s and 1880s, they were poorly received by the public. Most of them reviewed their own exploits without attracting attention to the brutality of slavery or the indignities being heaped on freed blacks by racial discrimination. An exception was three autobiographies of Frederick Douglass. As a former slave, he had more feeling for such issues.

Also an important factor in the decline of enthusiasm in the post-war abolition/anti-discrimination movement was the fact that the abolitionists were dying. By 1875, Gerrit Smith, Wendell Phillips, Samuel J. May, Beriah Green, Charles Sumner, Lewis Tappan, Jermain Wesley Loguen, and several others were dead. Their obituaries contained glowing eulogies of lives committed to others who were oppressed. Garrison said of Gerrit Smith,

> "...by reason of his intellectual and moral force, his munificent liberty, his rare self-abnegation, his stirring eloquence, his courageous and resplendent example, his personal gifts and graces, his all-embracing philanthropy, [he] made himself pre-eminent in the tremendous struggle for the abolition of slavery."[9]

The effect of this cooling of the abolition movement was the resurgence of racist attitudes nationwide. Even in liberal-minded upstate New York, the rise in such attitudes concerned local black leaders enough that they called in October of 1864 for a National Convention of Colored Men to meet in Syracuse to discuss rising post-emancipation levels of discrimination. Hosted by Syracuse abolitionist and underground railroad stationmaster Jermain Wesley Loguen, the agenda addressed the power of institutional discrimination through economic, political, and educational activity. This is an important level of discussion because it addresses a corrupt society instead of just the moral sinfulness of individual action.[10]

Writing to The Liberator in 1865, English philosopher and political economist John Stuart Mill recognized the significance of this institutional level of concern as he warned the country,

"One thing I hope will be considered absolutely necessary; to break altogether the power of the slaveholding
caste. Unless this is done, the abolition of slavery will
be merely nominal. If any aristocracy of ex-slaveholders
remain masters of the State Legislatures, they will be
able effectually to nullify a great part of the result which
has been so dearly bought by the blood of the free States.
They and their dependents must be effectually outnumbered at the polling places; which can only he effected
by the concession of full equality of political rights to
negroes..."[11]

Loguen and his colleagues realized this and had extended the
notion to the whole country. Their hope was that the vote would
give black people enough power to alter the crushing effect of institutional racism. But what they could not yet see clearly was the rabid
intent of millions of whites to maintain it. During the early days of
Reconstruction, Massachusetts journalist Russell Conwell visited
ten former Confederate states and reported regarding southerners'
homes:

"Portraits of Jeff Davis and [Robert E.] Lee hang in
all their parlors, decorated with Confederate flags.
Photographs of [John] Wilkes Booth [and] effigies of
Abraham Lincoln hanging by the neck... adorn their
drawing rooms."

He saw that the rebellion in the South "seems not to be dead yet."
Abolitionists may have assumed that northerners, having fought for
the emancipation of slaves, would carry the tide of equality to the
South. But even in the North, blacks' efforts were crushed by racism.

Northerners were afraid that increasing numbers of free blacks
would disrupt their caste-based position of superiority. They ac-

cused abolitionists of having tried to achieve their "ebony ideals" by ignoring northerners' vested interests. Shortly after the Civil War and the 13th Amendment had ended slavery, it became clear that racial <u>in</u>equality was what most white Americans expected and wanted. The northern mask of professional equality had been torn off to reveal the cultural hypocrisy of racist institutions.

It became obvious that the enormous efforts of abolitionists and soldiers had left the nation still mired in bigotry, as most citizens were unable to shed their racist thoughts and actions. Political and legislative remedies were too weak to forge an enduring equity, and in fact, only served to placate a publicly egalitarian but privately bigoted citizenry. This problem was epitomized in the Congressional impeachment and acquittal of President Andrew Johnson in late 1867. As Charles Sumner wrote, "Jefferson Davis was... in the casemates at Fortress Monroe, but Andrew Johnson was doing his [Davis'] work."[12]

Respected leaders in social and political realms had warned the American population of the possible effects of this bigotry if it lasted into the post-war years. As early as 1789, Benjamin Franklin had cautioned,

> "Slavery is such an atrocious debasement of human nature, that its very extirpation, if not performed with solicitous care, may sometimes open a source of serious evils."[13]

Henry David Thoreau warned over half a century later in 1854, just after the passage of the Kansas-Nebraska Act, "The law will never make men free; it is men who have got to make the law free." He concluded that freedom and equality depended not on "what kind of paper you drop into the ballot box once a year, but on what kind of man you drop from your chamber every morning."[14]

Boston orator and abolitionist Wendell Phillips' 1865 speech titled "The South Victorious" claimed that the South had won the war because of the power of continuing discrimination against free blacks. He lamented "all this forgetting—of the lessons of 30 years."[15]

Another Boston abolitionist and attorney, Richard H. Dana, went to a Faneuil Hall conference on Reconstruction goals in June of 1865. Dana delivered a speech in which he recognized the post-war choice regarding emancipated blacks:

> "Either you must have four millions [of] disfranchised, disarmed, untaught, landless, thriftless, non-producing, non-consuming, degraded men, or else you must have four millions of land-holding, industrious, arms-bearing and voting population."

The choice was clear: drop racial prejudice and enjoy social peace and equity, or keep it and expect the "war" to continue.[16]

By 1869 it was clear that the racist minds of Americans nation-wide had won the contest. Abolitionist Samuel J. May remarked,

> "The [former] slave-holders of our country and their partisans have been incomparably more vigilant in watching for whatever might affect the stability of their 'peculiar institution,' and far more adroit devising measures, and resolute in pressing them... than their opponents have been in behalf of Liberty."

As indicated also by the opening quotes of this chapter, the battle moved from the farm fields of Pennsylvania and Virginia to the Springfields of Massachusetts and Illinois as grass roots voters and their representative legislators endorsed white supremacy.[17]

In the landmark year of 1865, the Civil War ended, the 13th Amendment to the United States Constitution was ratified abolishing slavery—and the Ku Klux Klan was formed. As Lydia Maria Child had worried to Gerrit Smith,

> "Even should [the slaves] be emancipated,... everything <u>must</u> go wrong, if there is no heart or conscience on the subject."

As the war ended and the ethic of equality ebbed, the moral reformers lost out to the advent of practical and legal solutions to the enduring problems left by slavery. As most of the tired abolitionists withdrew from the public scene after 1870, they realized that military victory and political expediency could not bring about their long sought-after goals of racial equality. The *rules* of the social game had changed, but the *score* had not.[18]

The aging abolitionists held nostalgic reunions in the 1870s and 1880s. They passed resolutions in which they decried continuing discrimination, stating that their work would not be complete until blacks received "the political and civil rights of American citizens." They lamented, "Our work is not done."

Although attendees enjoyed their sense of community with old friends, they realized that the need for continued "moral agitation" against racial discrimination was not going to come from themselves, and that they probably could not inspire those born since the Civil War to care enough about it to carry on the fight.[19]

At their June 1874 reunion in Chicago, a letter from William Lloyd Garrison was read warning of the danger of "perpetuating caste distinctions by law." Two resolutions were passed encouraging abolitionists to continue active work regarding racial discrimination, but most of them had passed their prime time for action, and energy was low. At the April, 1875 meeting of the Pennsylvania Abolition Society, Dr. William Elder delivered an overview of the previous century of work by abolitionists. He railed that slavery had "bribed and bullied our politicians... dominated the press,... [and] profaned the pulpit."

The meeting emphasized the "counterrevolution" that was taking place against freedom for blacks because the American public seemed to be indifferent to growing racial prejudice. A letter from William Lloyd Garrison warned of the danger of historical amnesia, arguing that "the price of liberty is eternal vigilance."[20]

Lydia Maria Child summed up the post-war racial problem in 1879:

> "All our troubles originate in the fact that the American people, North or South, never really felt the enormous wickedness of slavery."

And because of this whitewash, they never felt committed to anything beyond legal emancipation.[21]

This post-war attitude was reflected in literature designed for public consumption. Magazines like Century, Harper's, and the Atlantic Monthly picked up on historians' efforts to reinterpret the Civil War as having been fought over states' rights or the preservation of the Union, thereby relegating abolitionists and their work to insignificance or irrelevance and helping to justify continued discrimination against blacks. Guilt over slavery was thus cleansed.

Articles published in the 1880s pictured the pre-war era as having been benevolent toward slaves with compassionate owners and happy "darkies" on plantations. Abolitionists were attacked as "indignant philanthropists" by former rebels, who emerged playing political and literary roles. Often the language used in such articles was a supposedly black dialect popular with readers, but it degraded "stupid" blacks.[22]

All of this fit well with the bias of northerners who believed that northern slavery had been a benevolent type—a "symbolic servitude" characterized by a "kitchen family." It all served well to perpetuate the racial discrimination that had caused slavery in the first place.[23]

Gerrit Smith's perspective on this post-war time period is typical of many of the crusading abolitionists, and underscores their feelings as they contemplated from "retirement" their gains as seen against their costs in time, effort, commitment, and—especially in Smith's case—money.

Smith thought that all of the political wrangling over interpretation of the Constitution, non-taxation of the South as a recovery measure after the war, the trial of Jefferson Davis, responsibility for the war, the enfranchisement of blacks, and reparation payments to the South only served to convince blacks that whites wanted to maintain control. Smith saw this white domination as a

> "dishonorable and treacherous spirit which... throws off the sense of moral obligation, when tempted to it by the prospect of advantage."

In the post-war era, this "advantage" was accruing to whites to the extent that it was setting the stage for future violence. Smith wrote to President Grant, calling his attention to the persistent withholding of "equal civil rights" from blacks.

> "To cease from this injustice... is the nation's first duty. The nation cannot be safe... if the discharge of this duty shall be delayed much longer."[24]

In agreement with Smith, acquaintances wrote also of fears of post-war discrimination. His housekeeper, Betsey Kelty, wrote in her journal on July 4, 1865 that before she died, she wanted to

> "hear the sound of universal <u>Emancipation</u>, that as a nation we may no longer claim to be free + independent with our foot on our Brother's Neck."

Smith's influence on her is clear here. She also recorded a few lines from a poem by abolitionist John Greenleaf Whittier:

"In vain the bells of war shall ring
Of triumphs and revenges,
While still is spared the evil thing
That severs and estranges."

In like fashion, Henry B. Stanton wrote to Smith,

"I am at time indignant, sad, discouraged, disgusted, at
the wicked + deplorable turn which events are taking
toward the Negro. Can it be possible that we have learnt
so little by this war?"

Smith agreed regarding the increasing tendency among whites
to discriminate against blacks.

"The lesson taught by our horrid War is Justice to the
Negro. A lesson costlier in treasure, tears and blood, was
never taught. And, yet, it remains unlearned."

He blamed long-term prejudice and threats to white status for
preventing the learning.

"After all [that this country] has done against the negro,
outraging and crushing him through the whole period
of her existence,... what is there left on which to base the
reasonable expectation that she will be just...? Nothing."[25]

In spite of this pessimistic view, Smith's attitude toward the
conquered South was conciliatory, as it had been from the beginning. He viewed northern acquiescence to slavery as an encourage-
ment to the South, and therefore saw equal responsibility for slavery
in both sections.

Shortly after the Civil War had started, Smith had told his
neighbors at a "War Meeting in Peterboro" that when the war was
over, the North should "be restrained from dealing revengefully"

with southern leaders. He repeated the theme in 1863, believing that concessions to the South would benefit the welfare of the entire country.

> "Notwithstanding their enormous crimes against their
> country... we shall gladly look upon our sorrowful Southern brethren as our brethren still."

Northern revenge, he felt, would only make national post-war recovery more difficult. More, it would ignore the humane point that the South had only done as the North had: it tried to preserve its values. To treat southerners as traitors would deny the point that citizens of a republic have the right to rebel. And, he claimed, because the South had been regarded during the war as a belligerent nation, treason was not applicable anyway. He believed that the South had suffered enough, and needed an embrace instead of a noose. The North, he felt, should be a role model of kindness to the world by treating the South

> "mildly and humanely! Thereby would we gain the
> respect and gratitude and love of the whole South....
> Moreover, a reasonable and human Peace, following this
> horrid war, would not only honor us in the sight of other
> nations, but it would contribute largely to advance the
> cause of civilization, and to elevate mankind, the earth
> over."[26]

One of Smith's fears regarding the post-war treatment of the South hinged on the untimely death of Abraham Lincoln. Lincoln was conciliatory toward the South, but his successor, Andrew Johnson, was not. Smith wrote to Johnson regarding his fear of the outcome of following "a vigorous and bloody policy toward the conquered rebels," and added, "it is apprehended that there may be qualities in yourself to which such a policy... would be entirely welcome." His advice to President Johnson was to be gentle, and not vengeful, toward the South. Smith received many letters from Virginia thanking him for his spirit of kindness to the South.[27]

Probably Smith's most compassionate act toward the postwar South was his paying of a portion of Confederate President Jefferson Davis' bail bond. Davis' physician while he was jailed at Fortress Monroe, VA was John J. Craven. He came to know Davis personally and wrote an extensive account of Davis' attitudes and experiences while in prison. Smith owned a copy of Craven's book (signed *Gerrit Smith, June 16, 1866*), and it is likely that its contents greatly influenced his philanthropic move to free Davis. Craven commented,

> "Is it not true that the chief... prejudices of public opinion come from our not understanding... the true motives... of the men to whom we are opposed...? History [will not] consent to regard Mr. Davis in the odious, monstrous, or contemptible light which has been... the only one in which the necessities and passions or our recent struggle would permit him to be presented to our age."

Davis, held in chains during part of his imprisonment, claimed:
> "...the laws guarantee certain privileges to persons held for trail. To hold me here for trial, under all the rigors of a condemned convict is not warranted by law [and] is revolting to the spirit of justice. In the political history of the world there is no parallel to my treatment."

Davis felt humiliated, and believed
> "...that the South should be restored its full rights in the Union and that it should be done quickly in order to avoid hatred developing out of vengeance. "

"Quarrels, between friends," Davis said, "are best healed when they are healed most promptly...."

As Smith read about Jefferson Davis' imprisonment, he certainly agreed with Craven's main point:

> "Make him a martyr and his memory is dangerous; treat him with the generosity of liberation, and he... will be a power for good in the future of peace and restored prosperity which we hope for the Southern States."[28]

While many in the North called for revenge and for Davis' head, Gerrit Smith saw the need for humaneness. Noting that Northern newspapers were upset with his signing of the bail bond, Smith printed a circular outlining his reasons for having done so. First, Smith said, it was cruel and unfair to hold a person in prison for two years without offering a trial; second, he felt a moral obligation to sign it, given his previously written positions on the war. The charge under which Davis was being held was treason. This, Smith said, was illogical: the war had not been waged under the rules of a constitution, but under the "law of war." To try Davis for treason would be to admit that the South had always remained a part of the nation. Smith warned Chief Justice Salmon P. Chase not to be trapped by this inconsistency.[29]

Smith viewed the vengeance being shown by the North as a heady abuse of the power of victory.

> "The shame of defeat is as nothing compared with the shame of abusing the power of success.... We may not recover so far from our passion and prejudice, as to be ashamed of this perfidy—but our children will be ashamed of it."

Perhaps Smith had been influenced by Elizabeth Cady Stanton, who had written to him in 1865 just after the war had ended,

"I feel for Lee + Davis very much... profound sympathy and respect.... I feel sorry to have Lincoln take possession of his house.... It seems so like trumpeting over a fallen foe."

The bail bond of $100,000 was signed on November 8, 1867 by Horace Greeley, Cornelius Vanderbilt, and Gerrit Smith, each of whom put up $25,000 while a group of others furnished the rest. Smith was confident that the act would show love and would lead to healing of wounds which were still open due to the failure of political action to sooth biases and aid reunification. Importantly, Smith was not attempting to forgive Davis for his crime of rebellion.

This act of signing Jefferson Davis' bail bond epitomized Smith's lifelong pattern of compassion for the oppressed. In this case, the oppressed included not just Davis, but also the slaveholders who were a continuing target of Northern vengeance; the former slaves who looked forward to at least ungrudging if not loving acceptance; the South, which needed its leader restored to dignity; and the whole country, which needed a solution to the divisive court issue of what to do with Davis.[30]

Although Smith's compassionate attitude toward the South did not represent the thoughts of all northerners, it carried significant weight among abolitionists, because he was one of the most powerful of that group. Garrison—another powerful leader—agreed with Smith, vowing that instead of being vengeful and cursing the South for having caused the war, northerners should bless the South with freedom and extend their best "love and good will."[31]

As the history of the era of Reconstruction and beyond indicates, the "love and good will" did not extend very far. Ku Klux Klanism, Jim Crow laws, and generalized racial prejudice in both the South and the North limited the life-chances of blacks. For example, when Frederick Douglass was away from his Rochester home in 1872, his house was burned. When he went there to be with his family, he was rejected at a local hotel because he was black. He responded by moving his family to Washington, D.C.

Four years later, Douglass delivered a keynote address at the unveiling of a monument in Washington designed to commemorate the emancipation of slaves. It depicted a standing Abraham Lincoln with his hand held over the head of a kneeling slave. It was obvious to Douglass that this was a degrading, paternalistic image of superior whites granting rights to blacks. He called it a "highly interesting object," and said to the mainly white crowd with President Grant presiding, "You are the children of Abraham Lincoln. We are at best his step-children."

Even during the twentieth century, segregation still held sway. At the dedication of the Lincoln Memorial in Washington on May 30, 1922, blacks were required to sit in a "colored section" to the side of the main congregation of people. In 1945, when black educator and United Nations statesman Ralph Bunche was working on some international projects, he was assured by whites working for him that they would "work like a nigger." And when his family dog died and his children wanted to bury it in the Washington, D.C. pet cemetery, they learned that there was a separate section for the pets of black people.[32]

Harpers magazine editor George W. Curtis wrote in 1867 that the South "will never be proud that ancestors of theirs fought heroically to perpetuate human slavery." He probably should have added that the North should also feel guilty for having fought so valiantly to achieve only the shallow victory of legal emancipation. As one Philadelphia freedman fighting discrimination noted, "this prejudice was akin to slavery."[33]

There are some signs in this early twenty-first century that racial discrimination is abating, but one wonders why Americans must refer to the election of Barack Obama to the presidency of the United States in 2008 in racial terms. He is consistently referred to as our first "black" or "African American" president. His parentage was of mixed races, yet we seem driven to call him "black," thus ignoring half of his biological background.

Philadelphia underground railroad station master William Still documented mixed-race breeding in the nineteenth century, recording a wide range in skin colors among runaway slaves. He concluded that the range of colors indicated long-term inter-racial breeding.[34]

Obviously, it still occurs. We still refer to most people with dark skin as 'black'. Perhaps even in a more progressive modern society, we cling to perceptions of a color line due to our continuing intent to discriminate.

~ Epilogue ~

I hope that reading this version of the history of the antislavery movement and the work of the abolitionists will remind us of the debt we owe to all those who have fought for freedom. Because control of and power over others is a perennial theme of social life, vigilance and courage in maintaining freedom are necessary.

The one percent of Americans who became abolitionists in the nineteenth century exhibited lifestyle contradictions that baffled most others, and thereby weakened their credence. They knew what they wanted to achieve and were stable and persistent in pursuing it, yet it appeared to many others that they were "crazy" or "mad" for upsetting tradition. They held utopian dreams, but often used practical means of pursuit. Their image in the public mind was both "inspiring and menacing" as they urged reforms that seemed to join heaven and earth, the sacred with the secular.[1]

Yet in spite of the paradoxes, the history of the antislavery movement should be inspiring to future generations. Its participants held their moral ground in the face of intense nationwide opposition, and created a network of influence to be envied by any who pursue social movements for change. The abolitionists are a beacon regarding democratic participation and self-empowerment. They touched everyone through the issues of race, political identity, morality, and responsibility.

Should the abolitionists be honored as social heroes, as were Civil War soldiers? Their "service" was not the result of enlistment for glory or bounty, but their call to moral duty resulted in a "thirty years war" that preceded and outlasted the physical conflict. They fought not for military victory, but for social triumph for all of humanity. And they did so in spite of the built-in headwinds of social bias against them.

Samuel J. May called the antislavery movement a second American Revolution—"The most glorious movement ever made in humanity's behalf." He felt that the names of its leaders should be as historically important as those of the founding fathers—or maybe even more so because the abolitionists fought for someone *else's* freedom. Most people, May said, were unwilling to risk as much as the abolitionists did, and would not "touch [abolitionism] with one of their fingers."[2]

Abolitionists like Gerrit Smith and Levi Coffin displayed the reform they sought by living unbiased, integrated lives. They modeled lives free of caste feelings; they did not separate black people from their own families—even transient ones. They helped some blacks along in their travels; others, they hired. They treated all with affection and acceptance. Yet because of the racist age in which they lived, perhaps none of them could envision the multicultural possibilities we strive for today. They had deep empathy for oppressed people, but their proposed solutions were often paternalistic. This was less a desire for supremacy than a symptom of an ethnocentric era.

As James Brewer Stewart has put it, they "explored the furthest possible boundaries of egalitarianism imaginable in their age."[3]

They were trapped by a cycle of events through which discrimination tended to reinforce itself. There was an opportunity to break the cycle without further discrimination or violence, but the general public avoided it. The cycle can be pictured as follows:

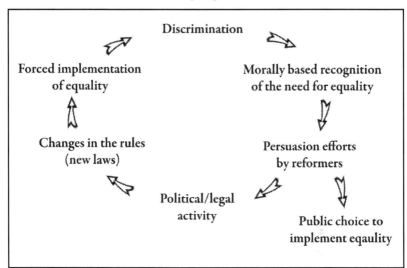

Although there are now many "civil rights" laws in place, racial discrimination persists. In sum, the abolitionists never achieved their ultimate goal, so work toward the abolition of discrimination continues today. Organizations like Antislavery International, the American Antislavery Group, and the National Abolition Hall of Fame & Museum fight against contemporary slavery and discrimination all over the world; still, 800,000 slaves are traded each year—many of them women and children.

And the Ku Klux Klan continues to grow. Between 2000-2005, the KKK experienced a 63-percent growth in the number of its chapters in the United States. Most of its new members are white males under 25 years old, and its targets are illegal immigrants, blacks, gays, and Jewish people.

In June 2007, the Democratic-dominated New York State Assembly passed a resolution "acknowledging that the institution of slavery was an appalling tragedy," apologizing for the part the state had played in slavery and recommending a "commemorative day in tribute to persons enslaved in New York State." The Republican-dominated New York State Senate refused to pass the bill.[4]

The tragedy of this story of the antislavery movement is that the machinery of government designed by our founders to ensure democratic decision-making amid the protection of minorities broke down in the face of a crisis built by self-interest. Pledges to fraternity and equality were eroded by passion, and brothers resorted to enormous bloodshed to settle the issue.

Today, there is a continuity of issues, goals, ideals, and methods that extends from Gerrit Smith and Frederick Douglass to the present. Their words and perspectives resonate in current efforts to advance freedom, justice, and civil rights. One can hope that the "era of responsibility" ushered in by President Barack Obama can bring some of these hopes to fruition.

Slavery was not the cause of racism; it was merely its manifestation. The hate, degradation, vilification, and denouncement of one race by another was carefully taught by a culture that is still with us. Discrimination against people of color remains as a contemporary form of tyranny, just as was slavery. It produces second-class citizenship for those who still must fight for their civil rights.

Just before his death in 1895, Frederick Douglass advised a young black man who had asked for his wisdom regarding a career, "Agitate! Agitate! Agitate!"[5]

The partial victory won by abolitionists, and by northern victory in the Civil War, will not have full meaning in American culture until we eliminate discrimination.

Perhaps we can follow the model established by Gerrit Smith, and pledge to do *whatever it takes* to finish that task.

Notes

Introduction
1. Mayer, 203, 445; Dumond, 225-226.
2. James G. Birney to Gerrit Smith, Sept. 13, 1835, SU.
3. Gerrit Smith to Elizabeth Smith, July 16, 1815; Sept. 3, 1817, SU; Kraditor, 168.
4. Harlow, 283-284; Oakes 92.
5. Baldwin, 22.

Chapter 1
1. Stauffer, The Black..., 36.
2. Filler, 30.
3. Goodheart, 21.
4. Higginson, 275, 276.
5. Dumond, 157.
6. Stewart, J. Abolitionist..., 90-94, 104-105; Mayer, 168.
7. Dumond, 158; Stewart, Abolitionist..., 9-12.
8. Singer, 91-91; Stauffer, Giants, 189, 391n.
9. Dumond, 151; Stauffer, presentation at National Endowment for the Humanities Teacher's Institute, Colgate University, July 31, 2008.

Chapter 2
1. Gerrit Smith to George H. Evans, July 29, 1844, SU; Hochschild, 93.
2. Dumond, 61; Letter, George Thompson to William Lloyd Gar-

rison, Oct. 22, 1835; Furnas 280-288.

3. The Liberator, Nov. 30, 1849.

4. Gerrit Smith speech in the New York State Capitol, March 1850; Gerrit Smith to Salmon P. Chase, Nov. 1, 1847, SU.

5. Gerrit Smith to Julia Griffiths, July 25, 1857, SU; Garrison quoted in Kraditor, 219-220; Gerrit Smith speech at Albany, March 13, 1856.

6. Dumond, 92.

7. Douglass, My Bondage..., 437.

8. Still, xiii; Jeffrey, Abolitionists..., 74, 81-82.

9. Lowance, 314-315; Weld, 9.

10. Lowance, 259; Douglass, My Bondage..., 416-417.

11. Douglass, My Bondage..., 464; Lowance, 259.

12. Sorin, 119-122.

13. Gerrit Smith to The Liberty Party of New Hampshire, March 18, 1846, SU; U.S. Department of the Interior, 15.

14. Dumond, 156-157, 175.

15. Storey, 38; Yellin, 30.

16. Perry, 114; Hunter, 4.

17. Speech of Gerrit Smith in Peterboro on the establishment of the New York State Anti-Slavery Society, Oct. 22, 1835, PHS.

18. Gerrit Smith to New York State Governor Washington Hunt, Feb. 20, 1852, SU; Stewart, J. Abolitionist..., 97.

19. As an example, see Kruczek-Aaron.

20. Stauffer, The Black..., 129.

21. Stewart, J. Abolitionist..., 63; Filler, 264; Hunter 83.

22. Mayer, 349.

23. Harrold, 45.

24. See Gerrit Smith papers, SU.

25. Kraditor, 236.

26. Mayer, 349.

27. Julia Griffiths to Mrs. Howitt, Oct. 6, 1852, in Frederick

Douglass' Paper, Oct. 15, 1852; Fladeland, 165.

Chapter 3

1. Stewart, L., 29.
2. Ibid., 31-36; Singer, 53.
3. Hochschild, 86.
4. Dann, When..., 60; Hunter, 96; Hochschild, 257-261; Miller, 41-45.
5. Filler, 13; Dillon, 7-8; Kashatus, 36-37; Newman, 16.
6. Dumond, 52; Harrold, 17.
7. Newman, The..., 18; Hamm, 2-5.
8. Filler, 14; Kashatus, 26; Newman, The..., 18.
9. Dumond, 53. Franklin was a convert to abolitionism, for in his earlier years he had regularly run ads in his Pennsylvania Gazette for the sale or capture of blacks, trafficked in slaves at his print shop, and owned slaves at his home. (Waldstreicher, 24, 25).
10. Smith, W.H., 36-37; Dumond, 97; Perry, 120.
11. Kashatus, 38-40; Sturge, 125, 127; Jeffrey, Abolitionists..., 43.
12. Hochschild, 5, 89.
13. Ibid., 99.
14. Franklin, 83; Miller, 121; Dumond, 28.
15. Dumond, 26; Freehling; Mayer, 168-170; Gerrit Smith to Salmon P. Chase, Nov. 1, 1847, SU.
16. Miller, 125, 131.
17. Newman, The..., 24; Kashatus, 10; Newman, The..., 29.
18. Stewart, L., 192, 193; Waldstreicher, 193; Hunter, 81; Harrold, 21; Dumond, 50; Stewart, L., 123.
19. Dumond, 16-24; Waldstreicher, 35.
20. Dumond, 133-157.
21. Dumond, 133-138, 158; Higginson, 123; Newman, The..., 109; Filler, 25; Abzug, Cosmos..., 134; Sklar, 322.

Chapter 4

1. Filler, 20; Dann, Practical..., 405.
2. Dann, Practical..., 405; Filler, 20.
3. Newman, The..., 110-111.
4. Friedman, 15; Newman, Freedom's..., 112-113, 187-191, 262.
5. Newman, The..., 99; Stauffer, The Black..., 154.
6. Newman, The..., 101.
7. Stauffer, The Black..., 98; Dann, Practical..., 410.
8. James G. Birney to Gerrit Smith, Nov. 14, 1834, SU.
9. DeCaro, 8; Newman, The..., 113.
10. Dann, Practical..., 408; Dumond, 171; Abzug, Cosmos..., 151, 154.
11. Gerrit Smith to Rev. James Smylie, Oct. 28, 1836, PHS; Gerrit Smith to Dr. Joseph Speed, Sept. 7, 1837, SU; Newman, The..., 114; Gerrit Smith to Washington Hunt, Feb. 20, 1852, SU; Wellman, 131.
12. Dumond, 129; Kraditor, 4; Filler, 61, 62; Gerrit Smith speech to the New York State Legislature, Feb. 28, 1856, SU.
13. Newman, The..., 117.
14. Stewart, L., 125-127; Newman, 33.
15. Newman, The..., 21, 23.
16. Filler, 14; Stewart, J., 22; Holy..., 22; Newman, The..., 125; Stewart, L., 125.
17. Newman, The..., 4-6, 18-19, 38; Phelan, 38, 65.
18. Newman, The..., 60-61, 70, 47, 58-59.
19. Dumond, 52-53, 95; Miller, 120.
20. Newman, The..., 31, 44, 87-95.

Chapter 5

1. The Liberator, Dec. 8, 1837; Newman, The..., 49-55, 84, 104-108.

2. Hochschild, 127-129; 63-64.

3. Stewart, J., Abolitionist..., 76-77.

4. Filler, 67-70; Gerrit Smith, "The Crime of the Abolitionists," Oct. 22, 1835, PHS.

5. Perry, 74; Kraditor, 237; Abzug, Cosmos..., 141-142.

6. Richards, 10; Hochschild, 324.

7. Sorin, 3.

8. Mayer, 112, 129.

9. Lowance, 160; Kraditor, 160; Abzug, Cosmos..., 130-135, 153.

10. Kraditor, 27; Oates, The Approaching..., 36; DeCaro, 6.

11. Gerrit Smith to Rev. James Smylie, Oct. 28, 1836, PHS; John Quincy Adams to Gerrit Smith, April 5, 1837, SU.

12. Stewart, J., Abolitionist..., 99.

13. Stewart, J., Wendell..., 126-132.

14. Wellman, 109; Mayer, 103.

15. Goodheart, 82.

16. May, 36-37; Mayer, 391.

17. Kraditor, 197-200; Mayer, 328; Gerrit Smith to Elizabeth Cady Stanton, Dec. 1, 1855, SU.

18. "Gerrit Smith's Constitutional Argument," The Liberator, Aug. 30, 1844.

19. Mayer, 125; Stewart, J., Abolitionist..., 83.

20. Bacon, 95, 99; Newman, The..., 127-128.

21. Mayer, 173-176; Perry, 121-124.

22. Mayer, 175-176.

23. Ibid., 174.

24. Newman, The..., 6-7, 131-151, 175; Stewart, J., Holy..., 141-142.

25. Hochschild, 196, 213-225, 347, 352.

26. Filler, 18-19; Storey, 37; Dumond, 46-48.

27. Oates, 37; Jeffrey, The Great..., 53-54; Mayer, 217, 230; Kraditor, 6; Dumond, 188-189.

28. Dumond, 183-189; Jeffrey, The Great..., 28.

29. Richards, 49, 158; Dumond, 178-179; Jeffrey, The Great..., 28.

30. Dumond, 153-156; Jeffrey, The Great..., 5-8, 18; Stewart, J., Holy..., 135-138; Stewart, J., Wendell..., 179.

31. Lowance, 292; Stowe to Gerrit Smith, Oct. 25, 1852, SU.

32. Stauffer, The Black..., 154; Franklin, 187; Harlow, 287; Abzug, Cosmos..., 141.

33. Julia Griffiths to Gerrit Smith, Nov. 24, 1851; Frederick Douglass to Gerrit Smith, May 1, 1851; April 12, 1856; May 23, 1856; Aug. 31, 1856; Dec. 16, 1856; Aug. 18, 1857; July 2, 1860; Sept. 8, 1862, SU.

34. Richards, 72; Goodheart, 75; Stewart, J., Holy..., 70.

35. The Liberator, Aug. 20, 1831, quoted in Jeffrey, The Great..., 14; Jeffrey, The Great..., 34; Hansen, 48-49; Sklar, 327.

36. Gerrit Smith letter to James G. Birney, May 11, 1839; Gerrit Smith letter to John T. Norton, Dec. 20, 1842, SU; The Liberator, Oct. 19, 1847; Jeffrey, The Great..., 2.

37. Jeffrey, The Great..., 36-54; Hansen, 50.

38. Perry, 156.

39. Harrold, 40.

40. Griffith, 24-25.

41. Allen, 2, 60-61; Dann, Practical..., 18.

42. Allen, 212, 213, 254.

43. Ibid., 252; Larsen, 252.

44. Harrold, 42; Jeffrey, The Great..., 41; Bogin, 10, 16.

45. Jeffrey, The Great..., 79.

46. Ibid., 18, 23; 1-13; Soderlund, 83; Bacon, 112.

47. Jeffrey, The Great..., 88-93; Stewart, J., Holy..., 83; Dillon, 102.

48. Dillon, 101; Dumond, 237-238; Kraditor, 6-7; Van Brockhoven, 197.

49. Gerrit Smith to Lewis Tappan, April 1, 1836; Elizabeth Smith Miller to Gerrit Smith, May 16, 1836; Dec. 23, 1836; Aug. 11, 1841; Gerrit Smith to Hon. Thomas Howell Buxton, June 13, 1839; Joseph Sturge to Gerrit Smith, June 13, 1839; William Jay to Gerrit Smith, July 12, 1836, SU.
50. Jeffrey, The Great..., 80-81.
51. Perry, 133; Kraditor, 42-43.
52. Weld, 196; Goodheart, 104-105; Gerrit Smith letter to Everett Brown, Aug. 9, 1872, PHS; Gerrit Smith letter to Susan B. Anthony, Dec. 30, 1868, SU.
53. Stewart, J., Wendell..., 285; Painter, 167.
54. Dumond, 226-227; Bacon, 67-70.
55. Richards, 121-125, 133.
56. Ibid., 168-170, 150.
57. Ibid., 48-49, 75-80.
58. Perry, 107; Stewart, J., Holy..., 65.
59. Mayer, 196.
60. Weld in Friend of Man, June 23, 1836.
61. Harlow, 284; Dann, Practical..., 448.
62. Richards, 43, 59, 94-95, 100; Perry, 138; Sperry, 59; Jeffrey, Abolitionists..., 40.
63. Stewart, J., Wendell..., 262; Filler, 267; Singer, 77, 81, 90.
64. Mayer, 148-149; Birney in Friend of Man, Sept. 1, 1836.
65. Gerrit Smith to Rev. Smylie, Oct. 28, 1836, PHS; Filler, 77; Jeffrey, Abolitionists..., 42; Abzug, Cosmos..., 143-145; Dumond, 349; Gerrit Smith speech, "The Two Unions," Oct. 28, 1862, SLC.
66. Richards, 34-36; Guelzo, 57.
67. Dann, When...
68. Fitzhugh, xix-xxi, xxii.
69. Franklin, 197-198; Hayden, 42; Desmond and Moore, 47, 87, 267-269.

70. Miller, 222; Bordewich, 21.

71. Guelzo, 19-20.

72. Larson, 142; Mayer, 196-197.

73. Smith, "The Crime..."; Third Annual Report of the American Anti-Slavery Society 1836, 17.

74. The Liberator, Aug. 14, 1857.

75. Kraditor, 163; Gerrit Smith to Rev. Smylie, Oct. 28, 1836, PHS.

76. Perry, 148-149.

77. Weld, 243.

78. Third Annual Report of the AASS, 1836, 17; Stewart, J., Wendell..., 159.

79. James G. Birney to Gerrit Smith, Sept. 13, 1835, SU.

80. Kraditor, 161, 23, 163.

81. Stewart, J., Wendell..., 196; Mayer, 520; Jeffrey, Abolitionists..., 191.

Chapter 6

1. Gerrit Smith, "To the People of the Town of Smithfield," March 15, 1843, MCHS; Gerrit Smith to Vice President Schuyler Colfax, May 14, 1870 SLC; The Liberator, March 12, 1847.

2. John Quincy Adams to Gerrit Smith, Feb., 1837, quoted in Stauffer, 30.

3. Gerrit Smith letter to Judge Nye, July 27, 1848, SU; Gerrit Smith to the editor of the Emancipator, Aug. 23, 1847, MCHS.

4. Gerrit Smith to John Thomas, Esq., Chairman of the Jerry Rescue Committee, Aug. 27, 1859, SU.

5. Kraditor, 120.

6. Stauffer, The Black..., 110-113.

7. Mayer, 428, 509-510.

8. Foner, Free Soil..., 147.

9. Stewart, J., Abolitionist..., 76; Gerrit Smith to William Good-

ell printed in The Liberator, Feb. 19, 1841; Gerrit Smith to Luther Myrick, Jan. 17, 1841, SU; William Seward, Feb. 19, 1842, SU; Abby Kelley, July 24, 1843, SU.

10. Storey, 101, 59.

11. Gerrit Smith to William Seward, Jan. 1, 1845, PHS; Broadside, "The Poor Man's Party," Oct. 17, 1846, PHS.

12. Quoted in Lowance, 309; Mayer, 344.

13. Storey, 97.

14. Wellman, Grass..., 152; Kraditor, 141; Dumond, 297.

15. Fladeland, 185.

16. Dumond, 297; Kraditor, 142; Gerrit Smith, "The Liberty Party," in Frederick Douglass' Paper, Dec. 11, 1851.

17. Gerrit Smith open letter to abolitionists, Liberty Herald, Dec. 7, 1843; Filler, 153.

18. Gerrit Smith, "The Liberty Party," Frederick Douglass' Paper, Dec. 11, 1851.

19. Dumond, 301; Stauffer, Giants..., 99; Gerrit Smith letter to George T. Downing, March 6, 1874, SLC.

20. Broadside: "Gerrit Smith to the Friends of the Slave in the Town of Smithfield," March 12, 1844, PHS.

21. Kraditor, 156; Kruczek-Aaron, 270.

22. Wellman, The Road..., 173; Kraditor, 153.

23. Dann, Practical..., 327; Oates, 111.

24. Dumond, 284-286.

25. Kraditor, 136.

26. Stewart, J., Abolitionist..., 52-55.

27. Goodheart, 92.

28. Douglass, My Bondage..., xviii; Stauffer, The Black....

29. Goodheart, 80.

30. Perry, 150, 191.

31. Friend of Man, Sept. 30, 1840, 4; The Liberator, Feb. 11, 1842; Bacon, 84-85.

32. Hunter, 223.

33. Hicks, et al., 559.

34. Blue, 17-23.

35. Ibid., 75-80.

36. Ibid., 119, 121; North Start, Aug. 11, 1848.

37. Blue, 120, 121.

38. Ibid., 144.

39. Storey, 62; Stewart, J., Holy..., 117; Richards, 163; Kraditor, 182-185.

40. Blue, 207-231, 241-247.

41. Dumond, 363; Blue, 280-281.

42. Storey, 108-109.

43. Hicks, et al., 608-610.

44. Mayer, 562, 510; Stauffer, Giants..., 191, 202, 306.

45. Storey, 231; Stewart, J., Holy..., 177-178.

46. Jeffrey, Abolitionists..., 193; Mayer, 456, 439.

Chapter 7

1. Stewart, J., Abolitionist..., 8.

2. Reynolds, 34; The Liberator, Nov. 10, 1837, 181.

3. Harlow, 108-109; Gerrit Smith to John Quincy Adams, July 16, 1839, SU.

4. Sperry, 60; Redpath, 238.

5. Dann, When..., 69; Dumond, 364.

6. Clinton, 84; Woodward and Muhlenfeld, 42.

7. DeCaro, 95; Franklin, From..., 198-199.

8. Hicks, Mowry and Burke, 551-556; Gerrit Smith speech in the New York State Legislature, March 13, 1856; Gerrit Smith speech "Denying Suffrage Even to Soldiers," April 20, 1863, SLC.

9. Hunter, 112.

10. Humphreys.

11. Dumond, 308-309.

12. Blue, 204; Dann, Practical..., 477-486; Bacon, 118.

13. National Era, Feb. 21, 1850; Blue, 201.

14. Sperry; Dann, Practical..., 468-469.

15. Stewart, J., Wendell..., 148.

16. Mayer, 406-407.

17. Sperry, 54.

18. Phelan, 173.

19. Syracuse Daily Standard, Sept. 24, 1850; Sept. 27, 1850.

20. "A Discourse by Wendell Phillips," The Liberator, Jan. 25, 1861; Lincoln quoted in Filler, 265.

21. Gerrit Smith to the New York State Vigilance Committee, March 14, 1849, SU; Harlow, 287; Stauffer, 195.

22. Lowance, 273.

23. Sperry, 55; Blockson, 193-194; Brandt, 69-75.

24. Stewart, J., Holy..., 162.

25. Stewart, J., Abolitionist..., 162-163.

26. Etcheson, 5-6; Gerrit Smith speech in the New York State Legislature, March 13, 1856, SLC.

27. Dumond, 192; Mayer, 447-448.

28. Redpath, 226.

29. DeCaro, 12-15.

30. Etcheson, 64-68; DeCaro, 48-50.

31. DeCaro, 50.

32. Reynolds, 138-205; Dann, Practical..., 491.

33. Etcheson, 37.

34. Ibid., 31.

35. Gerrit Smith, Speech in the New York State Capitol, March 11, 1850, MCHS.

36. Redpath, 233.

37. Ibid., 204-206.

38. Ibid., 190, 205-206.

39. DeCaro, 83.
40. Oates, 403.
41. Stewart, J., Abolitionist..., 168-169.
42. McKivigan and Leveille; Stauffer, 261-262.
43. Dillon, 264.
44. Redpath, 196, 281-282; Newman, Freedom's..., 112.
45. The Liberator, Jan. 25, 1861; Stewart, J., Wendell..., 219, 240-241; Gerrit Smith to President Lincoln, Aug. 31, 1861, SLC; Stauffer, Giants..., 231.
46. Guelzo, 64, 54-55.
47. Dumond, 372.
48. Gerrit Smith to his fellow citizens, Oct. 6, 1862, SU; Guelzo, 215-216; Stauffer, Giants..., 241-243.

Chapter 8

1. Mayer, 536.
2. Stewart, J., Holy..., 180; Guelzo, 65; Gerrit Smith to Montgomery Blair, April 5, 1862, SLC.
3. Mayer, 567.
4. Storey, 261, 270.
5. Ibid., 337.
6. Ibid., 335; Stauffer, Giants..., 400n; Gerrit Smith to William Lloyd Garrison and Wendell Phillips, Sept. 12, 1865, SLC.
7. Storey, 309; Jeffrey, Abolitionists..., 113; Gerrit Smith letter to Everett Brown, Aug. 9, 1872; Gerrit Smith to William Lloyd Garrison and Wendell Phillips, Sept. 12, 1865; Gerrit Smith to Horace Greeley, Oct. 1, 1872, SLC; Gerrit Smith, "To Thyself By True," Nov. 23, 1874, SLC.
8. Jeffrey, Abolitionists..., 17; Stewart, J., Wendell..., 265.
9. Jeffrey, Abolitionists..., 17, 165, 253, 109; Dann, Practical..., 563.
10. Franklin, 216.

11. The Liberator, June 30, 1865, 101.

12. Kumbardt, 34; Storey, 303.

13. Sparks, 515-516.

14. Mayer, 444.

15. Stewart, J., Wendell..., 268; Jeffrey, Abolitionists..., 56.

16. The Liberator, June 30, 1865, 101.

17. Jeffrey, Abolitionists..., 41.

18. Lydia Maria Child to Gerrit Smith, Jan. 7, 1862, SU.

19. Gara, "A Glorious Time," 290; Jeffrey, Abolitionists..., 203, 214.

20. Jeffrey, Abolitionists..., 105-108.

21. Ibid., 101, 102, 153.

22. Ibid., 222-223, 156-157, 160-161, 140.

23. Hodges, 204-207.

24. Gerrit Smith, "Jugglery," Dec. 20, 1867; Gerrit Smith, "No Treason in Civil War," June 8, 1865; Gerrit Smith to President Grant, March 6, 1873, SLC.

25. Henry B. Stanton to Gerrit Smith, Sept. 22, 1865; Gerrit Smith, "The Lesson Not Learned," March 25, 1868, SLC.

26. Gerrit Smith, "War Meeting in Peterboro," April 27, 1861; Gerrit Smith, "Speech on the Rebellion and the Draft," July 29, 1863; Gerrit Smith, "No Treason in Civil War," June 8, 1865, SLC.

27. Letter, Gerrit Smith to President Andrew Johnson, April 24, 1865, SU.

28. Craven, 195-198, 80, 248, 374-375.

29. Gerrit Smith to Salmon P. Chase, May 28, 1866, SU.

30. Gerrit Smith, "On the Bailing of Jefferson Davis," June 6, 1867; Elizabeth Cady Stanton to Gerrit Smith, April 10, 1865; Strode, 305, 309. The previous paragraphs were adapted from Dann, Practical..., 543ff.

31. Mayer, 559.

32. Stauffer, Giants..., 305-306, 311; Kumbardt, 36; Urquhart, 109, 137.

33. Jeffrey, Abolitionists..., 26, 81.

34. Ibid., 71.

Epilogue

1. Jeffrey, The Great..., 3; Abzug, Cosmos..., 3-8.

2. Jeffrey, Abolitionists..., 36-40.

3. Stewart, J., Holy..., 134.

4. ABC News report, May 22, 2007; CNN report, Feb. 7, 2007; Singer, 2.

5. Stauffer, Giants..., 314.

Bibliographic Note

The many letters used in documenting this research are not listed in the bibliography. Each letter is listed in the chapter endnotes, with its location referred to as follows:

MCHS – Madison County Historical Society

PHS – Peterboro Historical Society

SU – Syracuse University, Bird Library

SLC – bound volume of speeches, letters, and circulars in possession of the author. This volume will be donated to the Peterboro Historical Society.

Bibliography

Books

Abzug, Robert H. Cosmos Crumbling: American Reform and the Religious Imagination, New York: Oxford University Press, 1994.

Allen, Paula Gunn. The Sacred Hoop: Recovering the Feminine in American Indian Traditions, Boston: Beacon Press, 1986.

Bacon, Margaret Hope. But ONE Race: The Life of Robert Purvis, Albany: State University of New York Press, 2007.

Baldwin, James. The Fire Next Time, New York: Dell Publication, 1964.

Blockson, Charles. The Underground Railroad. New York: Prentice Hall, 1987.

Blue, Frederick J. The Free Soilers: Third Party Politics 1848-54, Chicago: University of Illinois Press, 1973.

Bogin, Ruth, and Jean Fagan Yellin, "Introduction," in Jean Fagan Yellin and John C. Van Horne, eds. The Abolitionist Sisterhood: Women's Political Culture in Antebellum America, Ithaca: Cornell University Press, 1994.

Bordewich, Fergus M. Washington: The Making of the American Capital, New York: Harper Collins, 2008.

Brandt, Nat. The Town that Started the Civil War, Syracuse: Syracuse University Press, 1990.

Clinton, Catherine. Harriet Tubman: The Road to Freedom, New York: Little, Brown and Company, 2004.

Craven, John J. Prison Life of Jefferson Davis, New York: Carleton, 1866.

Dann, Norman K. Practical Dreamer: Gerrit Smith and the Crusade for Social Reform, Hamilton: Log Cabin Books, 2009.

---- When We Get to Heaven: Runaway Slaves on the Road to Peterboro, Hamilton: Log Cabin Books, 2008.

DeCaro, Louis A. John Brown: The Cost of Freedom, New York: International Publishers, 2007.

Desmond, Adrian and James Moore. Darwin's Sacred Cause, Boston: Houghton Mifflin Harcourt, 2009.

Dillon, Merton L. The Abolitionists, New York: W.W. Norton & Company, 1974.

Douglass, Frederick. My Bondage and My Freedom, New York: Dover Publications, 1969. First published by Miller, Orton + Mulligan, 1855.

Dumond, Dwight Lowell. Antislavery: the Crusade for Freedom in America, New York: W.W. Norton, 1961.

Etcheson, Nicole. Bleeding Kansas: Contested Liberty in the Civil War Era, Lawrence: University Press of Kansas, 2004.

Filler, Louis. The Crusade Against Slavery, 1830-1860, New York: Harper + Row, 1960.

Fitzhugh, George. Cannibals All! or Slaves Without Masters, C. Vann Woodward, ed., Cambridge: Harvard University Press, 1960. Originally published in 1857.

Fladeland, Betty. James Gillespie Birney: Slaveholder to Abolitionist, Ithaca: Cornell University Press, 1955.

Foner, Eric. Free Soil, Free Labor, Free Men: The Ideology of the Republican Party Before the Civil War, Oxford: Oxford University Press, 1970.

Franklin, John Hope. From Slavery to Freedom: A History of Negro Americans, New York: Alfred A. Knopf, 1980.

Friedman, Lawrence J. Gregarious Saints: Self and Community in American Abolitionism, 1830-1870, Cambridge: Cambridge University Press, 1982.

Furnas, J.C. The Road to Harpers Ferry, Toronto: George J. McLeod, 1959.

Goodheart, Lawrence B. Abolitionist, Actuary, Atheist: Elizur Wright and the Reform Impulse, Ohio: Kent State University Press, 1990.

Griffith, Elizabeth. In Her Own Right: The Life of Elizabeth Cady Stanton, New York: Oxford University Press, 1984.

Guelzo, Allen C. Lincoln's Emancipation Proclamation: The End of Slavery in America, New York: Simon + Schuster, 2004.

Hamm, Thomas D. Untitled and unpublished paper on Quaker unity presented at the Friends of the Network to Freedom Association, Inc. Underground Railroad Conference, September 15-20, 2008, Philadelphia, PA.

Hansen, Debra Gold. "The Boston Female Anti-Slavery Society and the Limits of Gender Politics," in Jean F. Yellin and John C. Van Horne, eds. The Abolitionist Sisterhood, Ithaca: Cornell University Press, 1994.

Harrold, Stanley. American Abolitionists, Essex, England: Pearson Education Limited, 2001.

Hicks, John D., George E. Mowry, and Robert E. Burke. The Federal Union, 4th ed. Boston: Houghton Mifflin Company, 1964.

Higginson, Thomas Wentworth. Contemporaries, Boston: Houghton Mifflin and Company, 1899.

Hochschild, Adam. <u>Bury the Chains: Prophets and Rebels in the Fight to Free and Empire's Slaves</u>, Boston: Houghton Mifflin and Company, 2005.

Hodges, Graham R. <u>Slavery and Freedom in the Rural North</u>, Madison: Madison House Publishers, 1997.

Humphreys, High C. <u>"Agitate! Agitate! Agitate!" The Great Fugitive Slave Law Convention and its Rare Daguerreotype</u>, Oneida: Madison County Historical Society, 1994.

Hunter, Carol M. <u>To Set the Captives Free: Reverend Jermain Wesley Loguen and the Struggle for Freedom in Central New York, 1835-1872</u>, New York: Garland Publishing, Inc., 1993.

Jeffrey, Julie Roy. <u>Abolitionists Remember: Antislavery Autobiographies and the Unfinished Work of Emancipation</u>, Chapel Hill: University of North Carolina Press, 2008.

---- <u>The Great Silent Army of Abolitionism: Ordinary Women in the Antislavery Movement</u>, Chapel Hill: University of North Carolina Press, 1998.

Kashatus, William C. <u>Just Over the line: Chester County and the Underground Railroad</u>, University Park, Pennsylvania: Penn State University Press, 2002.

Kraditor, Aileen S. <u>Means and Ends in American Abolitionism: Garrison and His Critics on Strategy and Tactics, 1834-1850</u>, New York: Vintage Books, 1967.

Kruczek-Aaron, Hadley. "Struggling with Moral Authority: religion, Reform and Everyday Life in Nineteenth Century Smithfield, New York," unpublished dissertation, Syracuse University, 2007.

Larson, Kate Clifford. <u>Bound for the Promised Land: Harriet Tubman, Portrait of an American Hero</u>, New York: Ballantine Books, 2004.

Litwack, Leon F. "Slavery to Freedom," in <u>Slavery in American Society</u>, Richard D. Brown, ed. Lexington: D.C. Heath, 1969.

Lowance, Mason, ed. <u>Against Slavery: An Abolitionist Reader</u>, New York: Penguin Books, 2000.

Mabee, Carleton. <u>Black Freedom: The Nonviolent Abolitionists from 1830 Through the Civil War</u>, London: The Macmillan Company, 1970.

May, Samuel J. <u>Some Recollections of Our Anti-Slavery Conflict</u>, Miami: Mnemosyne publishing Company, 1969. Originally published in Boston, 1869.

Mayer, Henry. <u>All On Fire: William Lloyd Garrison and the Abolition of Slavery</u>, New York: St. Martin's Press, 1998.

Miller, John Chester. The Wolf by the Ears: Thomas Jefferson and Slavery, Charlottesville: University Press of Virginia. 1991.

Newman, Richard. Freedom's Prophet: Bishop Richard Allen, and the AME Church, and the Black Founding Fathers, New York: New York University press, 2008.

---- The Transformation of American Abolitionism: Fighting Slavery in the Early Republic, Chapel Hill: University of North Carolina Press, 2002.

Oakes, James. The Radical and the Republican: Frederick Douglass, Abraham Lincoln, and the Triumph of Antislavery Politics, New York: W.W. Norton & Company, 2007.

Oates, Stephen B. The Approaching Fury: Voices of the Storm, 1820-1861, New York: Harper Collins, 1997.

Painter, Nell Irvin. Sojourner Truth: A Life, A Symbol, New York: W.W. Norton, 1996.

Perry, Mark. Lift Up Thy Voice: The Grimké Family's Journey from Slaveholders to Civil Rights Leaders, New York: Penguin Books, 2001.

Phelan, Helene C. And Why Not Every Man? An Account of Slavery, the Underground Railroad, and the Road to Freedom in New York's Southern Tier, Interlaken: Heart of the Lakes Publishing, 1987.

Redpath, James. The Public Life of Capt. John Brown, Boston: Thayer and Eldridge, 1860.

Reynolds, David S. John Brown, Abolitionist: The Man Who Killed Slavery, Sparked the Civil War, and Seeded Civil Rights, New York: Alfred A. Knopf, 2005.

Richards, Leonard L. Gentlemen of Property and Standing: Anti-Abolition Mobs in Jacksonian America, New York: Oxford University Press, 1970.

Sellers, Charles G. "The Travail of Slavery" in Allen Weinstein and Frank Gatell, eds., American Negro Slavery, New York: Oxford University Press, 1968.

Sklar, Kathryn Kish. "Women Who Speak for an Entire nation: American and British Women as the World Anti-Slavery Convention, London, 1840," in The Abolitionist Sisterhood, Yellin and Van Horse, eds., Ithaca: Cornell University Press, 1994.

Singer, Alan J. New York and Slavery: Time to Teach the Truth, Albany: State University of New York Press, 2008.

Smith, William Henry. A Political History of Slavery, New York: Frederick Ungar, 1966. First published in 1903.

Soderlund, Jean R. "Priorities and Power: The Philadelphia Female Anti-Slavery Society," in The Abolitionist Sisterhood, Jean F. Yellin and John C. Van Horne, eds., Ithaca: Cornell University Press, 1994.

Sorin, Gerald. The New York Abolitionists: A Case Study of Political Radicalism, Westport, Connecticut: Greenwood, 1971.

Sparks, Jared, ed. The Works of Benjamin Franklin, vol. II. Boston: Hilliard, Gray, and Company, 1840.

Sperry, Earl E. The Jerry Rescue: October 1, 1851, Syracuse: Onondaga Historical Society, 1924.

Stampp, Kenneth M., ed. The Causes of the Civil War, 3rd revised ed. New York: Simon + Schuster, 1991.

Stauffer, John. Giants: The Parallel Lives of Frederick Douglass + Abraham Lincoln, New York: 12, 2008.

---- The Black Hearts of Men: Race, Religion, and Radical Reform in Nineteenth Century America, Cambridge: Harvard University Press, 2002.

Stewart, James Brewer. Abolitionist Politics and the Coming of the Civil War, Amherst: University of Massachusetts Press, 2008.

---- Holy Warriors: the Abolitionists and American Slavery, New York: Hill and Wang, 1976.

---- Wendell Phillips: Liberty's Hero, Baton Rouge: Louisiana State University Press, 1986.

Stewart, L. Lloyd. A Far Cry from Freedom: Gradual Abolition (1799-1827), Bloomington: Authorhouse, 2006.

Still, William. The Underground Railroad, New York: Arno Press, 1986. First published in 1872.

Storey, Moorfield. Charles Sumner, Boston: Houghton Mifflin and Company, 1900.

Sturge, Joseph. A Visit to the United States in 1841. London: Hamilton, Adams + Co., 1842. Reprinted by Augustus M. Kelley Publishers, New York, 1969.

Thompson, George. Letters and Addresses of George Thompson, New York: Negro Universities Press, 1969. Originally published in 1837.

Third Annual Report of the American Anti-Slavery Society, New York, 1836.

Urquhart, Brian. Ralph Bunche: An American Life, New York: W.W. Norton, 1993.

Van Broekhoven, Deborah B. "'Let Your Names be Enrolled': Method and Ideology in Women's Antislavery Petitioning," in Jean F. Yellin and John C. Van Horne, eds., The Abolitionist Sisterhood, Ithaca: Cornell University Press, 1994.

Waldstreicher, David. Runaway America: Benjamin Franklin, Slavery, and the American Revolution, New York: Hill and Wang, 2004.

Weld, Theodore Dwight. American Slavery As it Is: Testimony of a Thousand Witnesses, New York: The American Anti-Slavery Society, 1839.

Wellman, Judith. Grass Roots Reform in the Burned-Over District, New York: Garland Publishing, 2000.

---- The Road to Seneca Falls: Elizabeth Cady Stanton and the First Women's Rights Convention, Urbana: University of Illinois Press, 2004.

Wiltsie, Charles M., ed. David Walker's Appeal, New York: Hill and Wang, 1965.

Woodward, C. Vann and Elizabeth Muhlenfeld, eds. The Private Mary Chestnut: The Unpublished Civil War Diaries, New York: Oxford University Press, 1984.

Yellin, Jean Fagan, ed. Incidents in the Life of a Slave Girl, Written by Herself, Cambridge: Harvard University Press, 1987.

Periodicals

Colored American, May 23, 1840.

Emancipator, Aug. 23, 1847.

Frederick Douglass' Paper, Oct. 15, 1852.

Friend of Man, Sept. 30, 1840.

Gara, Larry. "A Glorious Time: The 1874 Abolitionist Reunion in Chicago," Journal of Illinois Historical Society, 65, Autumn, 1972, 280-292.

Hayden, Thomas. "What Darwin Didn't Know," Smithsonian, Feb. 2009, 40-48.

Kumbardt III, Philip B. "Lincoln's Contested Legacy," Smithsonian, February 2009, 32-38.

The Liberator, Aug. 20, 1831; Nov. 10, 1837; Dec. 8, 1837; Feb. 19, 1841; Feb. 11, 1842; Aug. 30, 1844; March 12, 1847; Oct. 19, 1847; Nov. 30, 1849; Aug. 14, 1857; Jan. 25, 1861; Jan. 30, 1865.

Liberty Herald, Dec. 7, 1843.

McKivigan, John R. and Madeleine Leveille. "The 'Black Dream' of Gerrit Smith, New York Abolitionist," Syracuse University Library Associates Courier, 20, Fall, 1985.

National Era, Feb. 21, 1850.

North Star, Aug. 11, 1848.

Syracuse Daily Standard, Sept. 24, 1850.

Index

Index

Index

Index

Index

Index

About the Author

Norman K. Dann, Ph.D. was born in Providence, RI in 1940. After graduating from Mt. Pleasant High School, he spent three years in the U.S. Navy as an aviation electronics technician.

He earned a bachelor of arts degree in psychology from Alderson-Broaddus College in Philippi, WV and a master of arts in Political Science from the University of Rhode Island.

He was graduated from Syracuse University in 1974 with a Ph.D. in Interdisciplinary Social Sciences. In 1999, he retired after 33 years on the faculty of the Social Sciences Department at Morrisville State College.

In retirement, Norm has specialized in research and writing on the abolition movement, with several articles and book reviews in publication. He published his first book, *When We Get to Heaven: Runaway Slaves on the Road to Peterboro*, in 2008. His second book in 2009 was a full biography that capped more than 15 years of research on abolitionist Gerrit Smith. It is titled *Practical Dreamer: Gerrit Smith and the Crusade for Social Reform*.

His fourth book, Cousins of Reform: Elizabeth Cady Stanton and Gerrit Smith, was published in 2013. His fifth book, Greene Smith and the WildLife: The Story of Peterboro's Avid Outdoorsman, was published in 2015. His sixth book, Ballots, Bloomers & Marmalade: The Life of Elizabeth Smith Miller, premiered in 2016. His seventh book, Peter Smith of Peterboro: Furs, Land and Anguish, appeared in 2018. His eighth book, God, Gerrit & Guidance: The Life of Ann Carroll Fitzhugh Smith, was published in 2019. His ninth book, published in 2021, is *Passionate Energies: The Gerrit and Ann Smith Family of Peterboro, New York Through a Century of Reform*.

Norm is a founding member of the National Abolition Hall of Fame & Museum in Peterboro, NY.

All of his books are available at logcabinbooks.com.